Don Miguel Ruiz,

With all my Love

& apprec

Wendy Lynne

I ♡ U !

Truth And Dare

A Journey of Creating and Daring to BE…
Who You Really Are!

WENDY LYNN

BALBOA.
PRESS

A DIVISION OF HAY HOUSE

ISBN: 978-1-4525-4376-5 (sc)
ISBN: 978-1-4525-4377-2 (e)
Library of Congress Control Number: 2011962328

Balboa Press books may be ordered through booksellers or by contacting:

Balboa Press
A Division of Hay House
1663 Liberty Drive
Bloomington, IN 47403
www.balboapress.com
1-(877) 407-4847

Because of the dynamic nature of the Internet, any web addresses or links contained in this book may have changed since publication and may no longer be valid. The views expressed in this work are solely those of the author and do not necessarily reflect the views of the publisher, and the publisher hereby disclaims any responsibility for them.

The author of this book does not dispense medical advice or prescribe the use of any technique as a form of treatment for physical, emotional, or medical problems without the advice of a physician, either directly or indirectly. The intent of the author is only to offer information of a general nature to help you in your quest for emotional and spiritual well-being. In the event you use any of the information in this book for yourself, which is your constitutional right, the author and the publisher assume no responsibility for your actions.

Printed in the United States of America

Balboa Press rev. date: 1/17/2012

Dedication

In Loving Memory Of

Timothy Joel Bergeron

3/23/60 – 2/7/10

I dedicate the Truth And Dare program to my brother-in-law Tim. With over 25 years of service in the Terrebonne Parish Sheriff's Office and many years of working with teens as a D.A.R.E. instructor, Tim was promoted to Major just after his untimely death, in the line of duty, in 2010. Tim was committed to teaching people how to live an honorable and respectable life. By example, Tim encouraged me, and countless others, to live an authentic, noble, and purpose driven Life.

Tim saw the good in me when I couldn't.
He believed in me when I wouldn't,
and
He loved me when I thought he shouldn't.

Timothy Joel Bergeron brought out the best in me and helped me bring the Truth And Dare program to Life. He found me worth his time, effort, and Love – so that I could find YOU worth my time, effort, and Love. I hope that the Truth And Dare program helps you to find Yourself, as well as others, worthy of all good things as well!

"People are like stained-glass windows. They sparkle and shine when the sun is out, but when the darkness sets in their true beauty is revealed only if there is light from within."

Elisabeth Kubler-Ross

"The best way to find yourself
is to lose yourself in the service of others."

Mohandas Gandhi

Acknowledgments

I am most thankful for my two boys, Austin and Dalton, who are
my inspiration and motivation to Be the best person I can Be. Thank
You both for being my Light through this Journey of Life.

I want to thank all the amazing teenagers who went through the Truth And Dare pilot
program for their commitment and advice during the program's development stages.

Special thanks to my best friends:

Kelli Fitzgerald Hartmann - who is my editor, advisor, and closest friend.

Shannon Rogers – who was my writing partner and sounding board.

Karen Peeler Wild - for being my marketing advisor and motivational support.

Donette Jumonville Freeman - who assisted in the editing process of the book
and who invited me to work with the amazing teens in her 2011 PSL classes.
The feedback and guidance of the teens in these classes had an incredible
impact on the effectiveness and design of the Truth And Dare program.

I would also like to acknowledge all the incredible authors and motivational figures/
speakers who have shared their wisdom with me and whose work has been a key factor in
my personal growth and Spiritual development. There are a few that I wish to mention
because their work is reflected in many of the dares in the program. I would encourage
people to look further into their work for more strength and wisdom: Wayne Dyer, Deepak
Chopra, Byron Katie, Neale Donald Walsch, Cheryl Richardson, Don Miguel Ruiz,
Robert Holden, Mike Robbins, Michael Neill, Marci Shimoff, and Gerald Jampolsky.

Last, but certainly not least, I want to express my over-whelming gratitude to
my husband Jesse Bergeron and our dear friends Paul and Lisa Daigrepont, who
supported me emotionally and financially through this whole process. Your patience,
encouragement, faith, and Love is what made the Truth And Dare program possible
and I am eternally grateful to you all for believing in me and the work I was doing.

"Live without pretending, Love without depending,
Listen without defending, and Speak without offending."

Drake

Contents

The Truth And Dare Emblem

The Truth And Dare Emblem depicts both the foundation from which the program was created, as well as the goal it aims to achieve.

<u>The Shield</u>: serves as a protective surface on which we define Who We Are and what we stand for.

<u>The Sword</u>: represents our commitment to seeking out, acknowledging, and accepting the **Truth** of Who We Are.

<u>The Bow and Arrow</u>: represents the action (**Dares**) required to live in accordance to the Truth once we have received It.

<u>The Light</u> that shines from behind the shield represents Who We Are.

<u>The Olive Branch</u>: represents the peace we achieve when Who We Are is perfectly aligned with the Truth and is visible in our actions.

This emblem was designed by the author, Wendy Lynn, and the person who this book is dedicated to... Timothy Bergeron. The graphic designer that brought this image to Life was Jeremy Cowthorn from *Look And Live Inspirational Designs*.

Chances are, you are most likely familiar with the age-old game of 'Truth or Dare'. If not, the game is easy. Each player begins their turn by asking any other player the simple question – Truth or Dare? If the player being asked the question chooses Truth, then they are asked another question in which they are required to answer truthfully. If the player chooses Dare, they are ordered to perform a certain action. Players who choose Truth are often called cowards or chickens. Whereas, players that choose Dare are seen as risk takers or daredevils. No matter which is chosen, the results often cause discomfort or embarrassment for everyone playing the game. Knowing this, one would think it would be difficult to get people to play. However, that is not the case! Teenagers and adults alike are often willing and excited to play a quick game of Truth or Dare.

Wait, I didn't tell you how to win. Truth is, I don't know! Truth or Dare doesn't have a clear set of rules or any definite instructions on how to play. Even odder, the goal of the game doesn't seem to be focused on winning at all. Instead, it tends to center on gaining or obtaining the approval of others by doing whatever you are told to do. With control constantly being switched from one player to another and embarrassment ultimately being the result of each turn, finishing the game with as little embarrassment as possible and protecting your reputation as best as you can seems to be the best a player can hope for. Even though it seems a bit odd and extremely risky to play a game where there is little to no chance of winning and so much to actually lose, people all over the world still do it.

As you can see, the title of this program, Truth And Dare, is only slightly different from the name of the game. Yet, changing the little word in the middle from 'or' to 'and' creates some major differences. Although the game and the program both focus on discovering the Truth and accomplishing Dares, the Truth And Dare program doesn't allow you to pick between being truthful or being daring. Even though neither have set rules or definite instructions, the age-old game evolves into an empowering program simply by challenging you to have the courage to choose both… Truth And Dare. However, the main difference between the game and the program lies in the opposing goals. In the game, the player's goal is to obtain the approval of others by trying to **appear** fearless. The goal of the individuals who go through the program is to obtain self approval by actually **being** fearless. When playing the game, the player's tend to focus on escaping embarrassment and protecting their reputation as best they can. For the individuals going through the program, their focus is on discovering and creating Who They Are instead of letting others determine who or what they become. Though the objective of the game is unclear, the program's objective is to help you reach your full potential in life by empowering you with the Self- Acceptance, Self-Respect, Self-Worth, and Self-Love that you desire and deserve.

Here are a few Truths that explain what the program is all about and why it was created:

"We are so accustomed to disguise ourselves to others that in the end we become disguised to ourselves." ~ François Duc de La Rochefoucauld

Truth is, Who We Really Are is far greater than anyone we can pretend to be. Yet, some people spend their whole lives hiding behind social masks just hoping to be accepted or loved by others. Unfortunately, we often disguise ourselves so much that Who We Really Are gets lost or forgotten along the way. Fear of rejection and feelings of not being good enough can quickly turn us into 'people pleasers' who value the approval of others over our own acceptance. As a result, who we are is often just a reflection of who others want us to be. Truth And Dare was created to empower you with the Self-Worth, Self-Esteem, and courage to remove your social masks and live your life for You! Ralph Waldo Emerson once said, "To be yourself in a world that is constantly trying to make you something else is the greatest accomplishment." Truth And Dare will help you to understand that there is no greater gift you can give to others, as well as yourself, than just to Be YourSelf. You will learn that the greatest benefit of Self Approval is that it allows you to appreciate having the approval of others without having a need for it. As you go through the program, you will discover that Being Yourself is not only the easiest way to live, but it is also the best way to live.

"The biggest room in the universe is the room for improvement; there's only one corner of the universe *you* can be certain of improving and that's your own self."~Aldous Huxley

Truth is, every day presents us with many opportunities for Self-improvement and personal growth. Too often, we miss these opportunities to better ourselves because we are more focused on trying to change or control what is happening outside of us instead of looking to better what is happening within us. There is a Hindu Proverb that states: "There is nothing noble about being superior to some other man. True nobility is in being superior to your previous self." Truth And Dare is an endless journey of Self-Improvement that focuses daily on BEING a better 'YOU' today... than the 'you' of yesterday. The program will encourage you to be accepting of who you are as you continue to become the Who You Want To Be. Along the journey, you will learn that life does not make you who you are; Life presents you with opportunities to decide Who You Are. Truth And Dare will teach you how to learn and grow from your experiences and relationships instead of being a victim of them. Although doing the dares in the program will improve your reputation, what becomes of your Character during the journey is an even greater benefit. Zig Ziglar once said, "What you get by achieving your goal is not as important as what you Become by achieving your goal." Truth And Dare is not just about doing good deeds, and it's not a behavior modification program either. This program simply exposes your power to create Your Self and challenges you to discover, define, and dare to Be the greatest You that You can BE. Ultimately, Who You Are and Who You Become is completely up to YOU.

"To think is easy. To act is difficult. To act as one thinks is most difficult."
~Johann Wolfgang von Goethe

Truth is, a person's intentions are often much better than what their actions will be. For the most part, people don't intend to fall short of their desired or best behavior – they just do. We may intend to do our homework and clean our room before going to bed, but we just never seem to get around to actually doing it. When our actions fail to accurately represent our best intentions, we tend to let ourselves, as well as others, down. On the other hand, when our actions support our good intentions, we feel good about Who We Are and can be proud of what we have done. Truth And Dare acts like a mirror; it allows you to see yourself as others see you so you can determine what changes or improvements you may want to make. The program encourages you to practice behaviors and develop habits that reflect your good intentions. It also allows you to eliminate behaviors that do not accurately represent the person you want to be by changing the thoughts and actions that produce those behaviors. When you align your actions with your good intentions, you can be proud of what you do… and of Who You Are.

"We have to learn to be our own best friends because we fall too easily into the trap of being our own worst enemies." ~Roderick Thorp

Truth is, no one in the world is more deserving of your respect, kindness, compassion, loyalty, forgiveness, and Love than YOU are! Yet, we often treat others far better than we treat ourselves. There is an African Proverb that states, "When there is no enemy within, the enemies outside cannot hurt you." Your Truth And Dare journey is all about accepting yourself as you are, loving yourself unconditionally, and creating yourself as the person You Are meant to Be. As you journey through the program, you will learn that the more you accept and love yourself as you are… the more likely others will be to accept and love you as well.

Although created as a Self-Empowerment coaching program, Truth And Dare is best described as a journey. Each step of the journey is filled with new discoveries (Truths) and life changing experiences (Dares). Like the game of Truth or Dare, the Truth And Dare program will take courage and the risks will sometimes be high. You will likely even experience feelings of fear and embarrassment when doing some of the dares. However, the Truth And Dare program will never ask you to do something that you don't want to do or that could hurt your reputation. Even though the program determines what needs to be done to accomplish the dares, you will be involved in the creation of the dares and ultimately can decide how you will accomplish them. The dares in the program are designed to bring out the best in you and allow you to be proud of what you have done even if it was a bit embarrassing or scary. If you are up for a challenge that will empower you and make you more like the person you always wanted to be, I Dare you to keep reading!

"The easiest thing in the world is to be You.
The most difficult thing to be is what other people want you to be.
Don't let them put you in that position."

Leo Buscaglia

"I don't know the key to success, but the key to
failure is trying to please everyone else."

Bill Cosby

Congratulations, you just took your first Dare! So, here is some good news. You will not spend much time reading this book. Truth and Dare has been designed to focus your energy on the dares and challenges. Less time reading will give you more time to accomplish the dares that empower you and re-create your character. There are ten short chapters. Each chapter focuses on a particular virtue or quality. For each virtue, you will be presented 6 dares. Each dare is designed exactly the same and uses a simple 3 part process (each part is equal to one page). The first part is the Truth page, and its goal is to raise your awareness around a specific Truth. The second part is the Dare creation page, and it allows you to create a dare that will help you to experience the benefits of that specific Truth. For all 6 dares, both the Truth page and the Dare creation page will be in the front of the chapter. **It is very important to complete the Dare creation page immediately after reading the Truth page.** The third part is the Reflection page, and it is where you will reflect on and record your accomplished dares. These pages are in the back of each chapter and should be done as soon as possible after you have accomplished the dare. At the end of each chapter, there is a chapter review and a couple of pages for notes.

Some dares will be easy; some will be hard. Challenge yourself to accomplish as many as you can - as often as you can. It is very important for you to understand that the results of the dares do not determine your success. There will be some dares that make you feel really good about what you have done because you got the desired result, but there will also be some that don't go the way you wanted them to go. As long as you have completed the actions required, you have successfully completed the dare. When you come across a dare that you are unable to accomplish for whatever reason, you can either replace it with something you think you can do or record how you would imagine the dare would have gone if you had actually done it. Try not to get upset with yourself if this happens. Like many things in life, practice is the key to success and changing old habits or unhealthy thinking often takes a little time. For every dare you accomplish, regardless of the result, acknowledge that you have done something good and allow yourself to be proud. As for the dares you don't take, there's always tomorrow!

The Truth And Dare program is all about YOU and was designed just for you! The purpose of the program is to provide you with the awareness, experiences, and encouragement to create Who You Are daily instead of letting others do it for you. The ultimate goal of the program is to help you reach your full potential in life by empowering you with the Self-Acceptance, Self-Respect, Self-Worth and Self-Love that you desire and deserve.

"Watch your thoughts, for they become words.
Watch your words, for they become actions.
Watch your actions, for they become habits.
Watch your habits, for they become character.
Watch your character, for it becomes your destiny."

CHAPTER 1

HONESTY

Honest: being free of deceit and untruthfulness; fair and just in character or behavior.

Dishonest: fraudulent or insincere.

As defined by *The Oxford illustrated Dictionary*

The Choice

Virtue: Honesty

or

Vice: Dishonesty

The greatest two benefits of being honest are:

1.) _____

2.) _____

The two most detrimental consequences of being dishonest are:

1.) _____

2.) _____

Honesty Agreement

I, _____, understand that being honest is more beneficial to me than being dishonest. Therefore, I agree to read the following chapter, answer the questions presented, complete any exercises, and attempt to accomplish as many dares as possible – as often as I can.

Signed: _____   Date: _____

Dare 1

"Many a man's reputation would not know his character if they met on the street."
~Elbert Hubbard, American writer and philosopher

In other words, if who others **think** you are was walking down the hall, and who you **really are** were to pass, they would probably not recognize one another.

Dare to be honest with yourself by examining your character.

Have you ever wondered, "How can they think that of me?" or "Why doesn't he/she like me?" Perhaps, a better question would be, "How am I 'showing up'?" As the quote explains, people often see us differently than we see ourselves. This is because we know our intentions and others only get to see our behaviors. Unfortunately, our actions or behaviors are often very different from our intentions. The fact that others perceive us differently than we perceive ourselves is a clear indication of this. So, what can you do? By examining how you 'show up' to others, you can identify what qualities you want to keep and which ones you really want to change. Truth is, you have the power to create a new you, simply by changing the things that you do. When a particular action or behavior does not accurately represent Who You Are or who you want to be, change it. We all have qualities that bring out the best in us as well as qualities that don't. Learning what they are is the first step to bridging the gap between who you appear to be - and who you want to be.

To accomplish this dare: Make a list of 10 qualities that best describe you. Choose 5 qualities that you really like about yourself or qualities you would like others to see in you. Then, choose 5 qualities that you don't particularly like. After you have completed your list, you will then choose one adult and two peers to provide you with an outsider's perspective. Ask each of them to list both your favorable and unfavorable qualities. Be sure to ask them to be honest in completing the exercise and assure them that you will not get upset at their responses. Let them know that you are making an attempt to better yourself through a careful examination into your personality or character, and their honesty will be appreciated and helpful.

Be Aware: It will not be easy to hear about your unfavorable qualities and you may not even believe that they are true. Try to detach emotionally from what you learn so you can honestly examine whether or not there is evidence to support what others think about you. Also, not everyone will agree on whether a quality is favorable or unfavorable. One person might think that being shy is an unfavorable quality and another person might think it is favorable one. Therefore, this dare is not about letting others persuade you to change Who You Are. This dare is intended to expose whether or not your actions represent the person you want to be and allow you to decide and define – Who You Really Are.

Honest	Loyal	Giving	Lazy	Patient	Funny
Disrespectful	Shy	Rude	Dependable	Greedy	Modest
Selfish	Dishonest	Outgoing	Optimistic	Respectful	Accepting
Judgmental	Conceited	Inspiring	Negative	Disloyal	Dedicated
Impatient	Forgiving	Vengeful	Considerate	Sociable	Thankful
Condescending	Inconsiderate	Unsociable	Unappreciative	Intelligent	Athletic

(You are NOT limited to the qualities in the box. Use any qualities that work for you)

What are 5 qualities that bring out the best in you?

1.)   2.)   3.)

4.)   5.)

What are 5 qualities that don't bring out the best in you?

1.)   2.)   3.)

4.)   5.)

Which quality do you hope others will use to describe you? _____

Which quality would you not want others to use when describing you? _____

What are 3 qualities you like in others? What are 3 qualities you dislike in others?

Like: _____/_____/_____

Dislike: _____/_____/_____

Which adult will you ask to help you accomplish this dare? _____

Which two friends will you ask to help you accomplish this dare?

_____/_____

I believe that I will find that my behaviors accurately represent me (hardly ever / not as often as I would like / sometimes / often / always).

Dare 2

"Honesty and transparency make you vulnerable. Be honest and transparent anyway."
~Mother Theresa

Dare to seek answers or advice from a reliable source.

Does it bother you when you hear an adult say, "Teens think they know everything?" Most likely, you probably don't think you know everything and you would willingly admit that there are many things that you are unsure of or may even be questioning. Often, it is very difficult to talk to someone about your concerns, personal issues, or to ask embarrassing questions. Being uncomfortable talking to an adult, parent, or even an older friend is very normal, but it is always better than avoiding the issue or seeking out answers from an unreliable source. You may believe that your parents, or other adults, wouldn't understand and have never had the experiences, feelings, or fears that you are having. Truth is, they probably have gone through the same experiences that you are currently going through, have had the same thoughts or fears as you do, and would understand if you gave them a chance! Everyone, at some point in their life, has had questions about what was going on with their body, was heartbroken a time or two, was scared, and was in need of help or advice from others. These can all be scary or uncomfortable situations filled with lots of emotions and fear, but they don't have to be! By seeking answers, help, or advice from a reliable and trustworthy source, you can gain the knowledge which they acquired from similar experiences, receive some support or encouragement, and maybe even avoid some undesirable consequences.

To accomplish this dare: Think of something that you are embarrassed to share but you would really like some advice on, help with, or information about. Perhaps you want to know more about sex, how your body is physically maturing, the effects and dangers of drugs, or how to have a healthy relationship with someone. Maybe you want to discuss some religious concerns or fears that you have with someone who may understand. Most adults have experienced not just one of these, but all of them. By having an open line of communication with an adult, you can benefit from their knowledge and experience. If this seems too hard at first, start with small conversations about something that is bothering you, a problem you are having with a friend, or even something that you are happy about.

Be Aware: This may surprise you, but the parent or adult you choose may be just as embarrassed or nervous about talking to you about sensitive topics as you are with them. Most likely though, they will still be very glad you came to them and will be very willing to help. This dare is not solely designed to provide you with answers or guidance. The main focus of the dare is to encourage you to seek and establish an open relationship with an adult who you trust and feel comfortable with so you can go to them with your questions and concerns.

What are your initial feelings about doing this dare? _____

_____

What are some possible topics you have questions, concerns, or even just want to discuss with someone who may help? Try to list one **concern** (perhaps health or relationship), one **question** (religion/sex/values), and one **emotional situation** (upset about something / fears / pain). Consider who would be a reliable and trustworthy source with whom you would be most comfortable talking to about for each particular issue. It must be someone you trust and feel comfortable with – otherwise the dare may go unaccomplished.

1.) **Concern**: _____

_____

Who would you choose to talk to about this? _____

2.) **Question**: _____

_____

Who would you choose to talk to about this? _____

3.) **Emotional situation**: _____

_____

Who would you choose to talk to about this? _____

How do you think the person you have chosen will respond to your openness and

willingness to communicate with them? _____

_____

What sometimes stops you from getting advice, answers, or help from adults? _____

_____

What concerns, questions, or fears seem to come up most often for you? _____

_____

Try to have at least one conversation from your list.

Dare 3

"**A friend is a person with whom I may be sincere. Before him I may think aloud.**"
~ Ralph Waldo Emerson
American poet and philosopher

Dare to be honest with your friends and family by telling them what they do or say that bothers you.

Can you think of something a friend or family member does that bothers you? Is there anything in particular that they often say to you or about you which really gets under your skin? Unfortunately, our friends and family members often remain unaware of the things they do or say that bothers us because we never actually tell them. What do you suppose keeps us from telling them about the things they do or say that makes us mad or hurts us? Did you think of fear? Fear probably is the most common reason why we aren't honest with others when it comes to these things. Being afraid of how they will respond to what we tell them or how our honesty may damage the relationship will likely prevent us from ever telling the people we care about how we really feel. Have you ever considered how keeping your feelings hidden affects both you and the relationship? Truth is, suppressing your feelings is frequently more damaging than expressing them would be. The people you care about deserve to know how you feel and probably want to know when they do or say something that bothers you or hurts you. Wouldn't you want to know? Being willing and able to communicate how you feel with the people who are important in your life will help you to build stronger, healthier, and longer-lasting relationships.

To accomplish this dare: Dare yourself to tell a friend or family member what they do or say that bothers, upsets, or hurts you. How you approach the conversation is a key element for accomplishing this dare with love and respect for the other person. Whenever you are expressing a negative feeling or comment, it is important to say something positive first. This is not necessarily a way to lessen the blow as much as it is a way to express that you value and honor the person and the relationship. Let them know that you are being honest with them because you want the friendship or relationship to be the best it can be.

Be Aware: This dare may <u>appear</u> to be an attempt to change or control another's behavior, but it is not! The dare is simply an exercise in honesty designed to encourage you to express to others what bothers, hurts, or upsets you. How the person responds and whether or not they change their behavior is ultimately out of your control. However, you can control how you respond to whatever results come from your honesty and determine what **you** can, should, or will do about them. So, it would be wise to consider what response would be most beneficial to you and the relationship if they get mad at you or their behavior doesn't change. Be prepared for the worst, but expect the best.

What is your initial feeling about this dare? _____

_____

Can you recall a time where you have expressed to someone what they do that bothers or aggravates you? YES / NO

If Yes, what was the result? _____

Would you want a friend to tell you what you do that bothers them?   YES or NO

On line 1, list 2 friends or family members who you might want to accomplish this dare with.

On line 2, list at least one quality you **love** about them.

On line 3, explain what they do that upsets you or just gets under your skin.

    1.) a. _____   b. _____

    2.) a. _____   b. _____

    3.) a. _____

        b. _____

How do you suppose person "a" would respond? _____

How do you suppose person "b" would respond? _____

Do you think that person "a" would find it (easy or difficult) to change the behavior?

Do you think that person "b" would find it (easy or difficult) to change the behavior?

Person (a / b) would probably be more willing and able to change their behavior.

Describe how you feel when these people do those behaviors? _____

_____

What can you do to change how you react or feel if the behavior persists? _____

_____

One benefit of being honest about the things that bother, hurt or upset me would be

_____

Dare 4

"A lie gets halfway around the world before the truth has a chance to get its pants on."
~Sir Winston Churchill

Dare to speak only what you know is true.

"Just the facts please!" On any given day, you would likely be very surprised if you were to discover how little of what is spoken is actually true. Most of the things that people speak are really only their subjective opinions or personal beliefs presented as if they were actually facts. What is even more shocking is how willing and quick people are to believe what they hear without even thinking about it or questioning what makes it true. Have you ever thought about how easy it is to accept something as true? It can be as easy as, you hear it…you believe it…and then you repeat it! Unfortunately, if it isn't true (which is often the case) you are both believing and spreading a lie. Truth is, to only speak what is true… you must first know what is true. Seeking out what is true and checking the facts before you repeat things makes you less likely to believe or spread a lie. If we repeat something we heard from a trusted friend and it turned out to be false, we look like a liar. Even though we didn't lie, whoever we told sees us as the source of the lie because we are the one who they heard it from. For example, your good friend Gina tells you that there will be a pop quiz in math class today. You tell 3 friends, who all decide to spend their entire lunch preparing for it. You get to class and guess what? No quiz! Who do you think your 3 friends will be mad at? Yet, if you would have said, "I heard that there may be a pop quiz in math today, but I am not certain if it's true," they would probably appreciate you telling them even if they didn't have a quiz. When there is no way to know if something you are about to say is true, you can still be honest by acknowledging or identifying what you say for what it is. If it's an opinion, say it's an opinion. If it is hearsay, say it is hearsay. If you believe something to be true from your experience, you can say, "From my experience, this is what I believe to be true." You can even use the words "I believe" or "I think" to avoid presenting something as a fact when you are not certain that it is. By doing this, you can remain honest even if what you're saying isn't absolutely or completely true.

To accomplish this dare: Speak only what you know is true for 2 consecutive days. The easiest way to do this is to **acknowledge or identify** almost everything you say for what it is. Avoid lying, stating opinions as facts, exaggerating, and repeating what you have been told unless you know for certain it is true. This will be very hard to do and may take time to accomplish. So, don't be too hard on yourself because most adults would probably find this dare almost impossible to do as well.

Before attempting to accomplish this dare, take one day to notice how much of what you say is true, how much of it could be false, and how much of it is hearsay. At the end of the day, answer the questions on the following page.

I noticed that the things I say are most often (facts / opinions / hearsay).

I noticed that much of what others say is most often (facts / opinions / hearsay).

I (never / rarely / sometimes / often / always) accept what others say as true without questioning why it is true.

I (always / often / sometimes / rarely / never) repeat things without checking to see if they are true first.

Did you notice others repeating what they heard without checking the facts first? Yes / No

Do you ever find yourself saying silly things just to be a part of the conversation? Yes / No

Do you sometimes exaggerate or make things up? Yes / No If yes, why do you suppose

you feel a need to do so? _____

_____

Avoiding (lying / stating my opinions as facts / exaggerating / repeating what I heard without finding out first if it is true) will be the hardest part of accomplishing this dare.

What do you think is the greatest benefit of acknowledging or identifying what you say as

what it is? _____

_____

Food for Thought: Sometimes, it is easy to tell if someone is lying, exaggerating, or stating an opinion as if it were a fact. Other times, it is very hard to tell. The best way to discover the Truth is to keep asking questions until you are convinced that you have found it. Here are a few examples of questions that can help you get a more honest answer than the one you have been given. When asked at just the right time and in the most appropriate manner, these questions may even encourage others to seek and speak only what is true.

How true is that?

Are you certain about that?

Do you absolutely **know** that to be true?

Is that your opinion or a fact?

Could you be wrong about that?

What evidence would you use to support that?

Is that an assumption or a fact?

Did someone tell you that or do you know from your own experience?

★★★Try to use at least 2 of the above questions while accomplishing this dare.★★★

Dare 5

"There can be no friendship without confidence, and no confidence without honesty."

~Dr. Samuel Johnson

Dare to let someone know how they have hurt you.

There will be times when people's words or actions really hurt us. When this happens, we can get angry, disappointed, emotionally withdraw, or even become spiteful. Talking about what happened or how you feel is usually **not** how most people handle it. When someone hurts us or does something that makes us angry, we often keep it to ourselves. The major problem with this is that we don't let it go. Sometimes it eats at us so much and for so long that it ends up damaging or destroying the relationship. Truth is, we are often hurt the most by the people we love the most and who would never intentionally do anything to hurt us. Unfortunately, we often assume they meant to hurt us or believe they should have known better, even when they didn't. Imagine you told someone you trusted that you liked a particular boy/girl. When you told them, you never really came out and said, "Don't tell anyone!" Perhaps you thought they knew not to tell. Then, at lunchtime, the name of the person you like comes up and your trusted friend casually says, "That's who (your name) thinks is cute." Now, you are boiling with anger but you never say anything. Technically, your trusted friend never meant to hurt you and didn't really do anything wrong. That doesn't change the fact that you are as mad as you can be. By telling that person, "I really didn't want you to tell anyone, and I am really mad that you did," you give them the opportunity to say they are sorry, explain what their intention was, and perhaps think of a way to make things better. Honestly, they deserve the chance to explain or defend themselves just as much as you deserve to hear it.

To accomplish this dare: Let someone know what they did or didn't do that really hurt you. Think of a time when you were let down, hurt, or mistreated by someone close to you but decided to keep it to yourself. Maybe you found out they were talking behind your back, betrayed your trust by sharing a secret, or perhaps they weren't there for you when you needed them the most. Take some time to think about what you want to say and then talk to them about it in a respectful and compassionate manner. The goal of the dare is to be honest, get your feelings out in the open, and allow the person the opportunity to explain what their intention was or apologize if they want to.

Be Aware: The goal of this dare is not to make the other person feel guilty; the goal is to make you both feel better. Ideally, the dare will help **you** to release any harmful emotions that may be lingering or damaging the relationship by having the courage to communicate how you feel to the person who has hurt you.

Do you usually consider whether it was intentional or unintentional when you are hurt, betrayed, or disappointed by someone close to you?   Yes / No

I found it (easy / hard) to think of a person or occurrence that would allow me to accomplish this dare.

Who is the person you will talk to and express how they have hurt you? _____

Briefly describe what they did and how it made you feel: _____

_____

_____

Do you think their intention was to hurt you? Yes / No / Not sure

How do you think they will respond? _____

How would you like to feel after the conversation? _____

What would have to happen for you to feel that way? _____

_____

Does it ease your pain or lessen your anger when the other person feels guilty? Yes / No

Food for Thought:

Have you ever gotten angry at someone for talking bad about you? Yes / No

Have you ever been hurt because someone you trusted betrayed your trust? Yes / No

Have you ever felt put down or insulted by someone close to you? Yes / No

Have you ever had a friend turn their back on you when you needed them? Yes / No

Truth is, the things that upset or anger us the most are things that **we do as well**. Can you honestly say that you have not spoken poorly of a friend behind their back, shared a secret, or threw an insult out when you weren't thinking clearly? The next time you are hurt or get mad, consider whether or not you have ever done the same thing and whether it was your intention to be hurtful.

Remember: It is not wise to throw stones if you live in a glass house!

Dare 6

"There is only one way to achieve happiness…, and that is to have a clear conscience or none at all."

~Oqden Nash, American Poet

"The best tranquilizer is a clear conscience."

~ Benjamin Franklin

Dare yourself to confess something you already got away with!

When the Truth is something we don't want others to know or we fear that there will be negative consequences for something we have done, being honest will not be easy and often takes more courage than we can find. So, we decide to either make up a lie, or we try to hide the Truth. Sometimes we get away with being dishonest and sometimes we don't. However, just because nobody finds out what we have done doesn't mean we have actually gotten away with it. Truth is, living with the guilt or regret of what we did is often worse than the consequences that being honest may have caused. Telling little white lies that really don't hurt anyone will probably not make us feel too guilty or cause us to regret what we have done enough to confess them. Breaking rules that we don't agree with or that restrict our fun will likely cause a little guilt when we are breaking them but not so much that we can't live with it. But, when we do something that goes against our values or principles, our conscience will create feelings of guilt and regret that can be extremely hard to live with. By practicing being honest, you actually make it easier to live with yourself.

To accomplish this dare: There are 3 ways to accomplish this dare.

1.) Confess 5 'little white lies'. Perhaps you told a friend you got an A on a test when you really got a C. You could say, "I am sorry I lied. I just didn't want you to think I was not as smart as you."

2.) Confess 3 'broken rules'. "Mom, I know you told me not to eat in my room, but the other day when you were at the store – I did. I am sorry."

3.) Confess 1 'serious regret'. If you find the courage to do this one, it may be helpful to use a sentence that starts like this: "I know that telling you the truth is going to get me in a lot of trouble, but I want to do what I know is right and try to even make things right." Confessing to cheating on a test, stealing, vandalism, sneaking out, under-aged drinking, doing illegal drugs, or anything you think might get you in trouble will do.

Be Aware: You might regret accomplishing this dare if it causes you to get in trouble. If you do regret it, you missed the whole point of the dare and haven't yet learned the value or benefits of being honest. Also, sometimes people know what we have done and have not told us they know. In these cases, they have either let it go, are still harboring it, or were not affected by it as much as we thought they would be. However, even if there are no negative consequences, you still get credit for doing the dare.

I (always / often / sometimes / rarely / never) make up little white lies.

I (always / often / sometimes / rarely / never) break the rules at home or at school.

What is 1 serious regret that you could confess? _____

_____

Do you feel guilty for this action? Yes / No   Can You live with the guilt? Yes / No

How might the person/people you would have to confess to respond to the Truth?

_____

What may be the consequence of confessing this? _____

_____

Would you be able to live with that? Yes / No

How can confessing what you have done benefit you? _____

_____

What rules do you often get away with breaking? _____

_____

How does confessing something you are not proud of make you feel? _____

_____

I would have to say that fear of (rejection / punishment / embarrassment / hurting others feelings / _____) is what causes me to lie or hide the Truth most often.

I will accomplish this dare by confessing (5 white lies / 3 broken rules / 1 serious regret).

Food for Thought: Sometimes rules or restrictions exist for reasons that are unknown or not understood by the person who is expected to keep them. Have you ever had to abide by a rule that didn't make sense to you or just seemed silly? For example, a "No Trespassing" sign was just posted on the lot that you and your friends play ball on every Sunday. You assume that the owner is just trying to sabotage your fun because he is a grumpy old man. The truth might be that he discovered the lot was infested with red ants and had someone come out earlier that day to spray the grass with poison. He actually enjoys watching you and your friends play ball and wanted to provide you with a safe field that would be free of ants. Try to consider or inquire into the reasons for the rules that you don't understand or seem unfair before you decide to break them.

ACCOMPLISHED
Honesty Dare 1

The 3 people who helped me accomplish this dare was:

Adult: _____

2 Friends: _____ / _____

I learned that my 3 most favorable qualities are:

1.) _____

2.) _____

3.) _____

I learned that my least 3 favorable qualities are:

1.) _____

2.) _____

3.) _____

I was shocked to find out that I am sometimes seen as being _____

I am proud that I am often seen as being _____

My favorite quality is _____

I intend to work on improving _____

I am glad I did this dare because _____

_____

I think this dare should be done (just once / sometimes / often)

CONGRATULATIONS ON YOUR SUCCESS

ACCOMPLISHED
Honesty Dare 2

I accomplish this dare by talking to _____

about _____

Before the conversation I felt _____

During the conversation I felt _____

After the conversation I felt _____

What I learned was _____

_____

The person I spoke with had similar experiences, fears, or feelings as I did when they were my age. True / False

The person I spoke with seemed _____ that I spoke to them about this issue.

Another person who might have been able to help is _____

Another topic I would like answers about is: _____

_____

I (learned a little / got good advice / was still confused) about the topic we discussed.

I would be (more likely / still a little shy / not likely) to talk about this again.

What do you think would be the biggest benefit in having an open line of

communication with a trusted adult? _____

_____

CONGRATULATIONS ON YOUR SUCCESS

Honesty Dare 3

I accomplished this dare by talking to _____

about _____

How did you feel during the conversation? _____

How did they respond to what you told them? _____

_____

What was the outcome of the conversation? _____

_____

_____

Were any apologies exchanged? Yes / No

I believe the person will: (circle the statement that seems most reasonable)

- try to change the behavior
- try not to do the behavior in front of me
- attempt to change it but might take some time to do so
- pretend I never told them
- continue the behavior because they don't want to change it
- continue the behavior intentionally to hurt me
- choose not to be my friend anymore

What will you do or how will you respond if the behavior isn't changed? _____

_____

The most important thing I learned or want to remember from this dare is _____

_____

CONGRATULATIONS ON YOUR SUCCESS

Honesty Dare 4

Accomplishing this dare was: (very difficult / somewhat difficult / more difficult than I thought it would be / somewhat easy / very easy)

The hardest part was _____

What positive and/or negative feelings came up for you while trying to accomplish the dare?

_____

_____

It was (very difficult / somewhat difficult / somewhat easy / very easy) to acknowledge and identify what I was saying as an opinion, fact, hearsay, personal experience, belief or thought.

I found that others (never / rarely / sometimes / often / always) acknowledge and identify what they say as an opinion, fact, hearsay, personal experience, belief or thought.

Did you attempt to encourage others to seek and speak only what is true by using the example questions? Yes / No   If Yes, what responses did you get?

_____

_____

The most important thing I learned from this dare was _____

_____

It is (very / somewhat / not) important to me that people know they can trust what I say and believe me to be an honest person.

I am (not likely / not as likely as I would like to be / somewhat likely / very likely) to continue practicing this dare.

CONGRATULATIONS ON YOUR SUCCESS

1   HONESTY

Honesty Dare 5

I accomplished this dare by talking to _____

about _____

What was their reaction? (surprised / angry / confused / sad / _____)

What was the person's response? _____

_____

Were there any apologies exchanged? Yes / No

Do you believe that the person's intention was to hurt you? Yes / No

How did it make you feel to talk with them about it? _____

_____

List 2 things that make you mad or really hurt you when others do it to you but you also sometimes do the same thing to others.

_____

_____

Do you think that this dare will cause you to consider other's intentions as well as your own behaviors the next time you feel hurt or angry as a result of someone's behavior or words? Yes / No

The most important thing I learned from this dare is _____

_____

CONGRATULATIONS ON YOUR SUCCESS

Honesty Dare 6

If you did 5 little white lies or 3 broken rules, use the confession that was the most difficult for you to complete this page.

I accomplished this dare by confessing _____

_____

How did confessing the Truth make you feel? _____

_____

How did the person you confessed to feel about the Truth? How did they react? _____

_____

What was the person's response? _____

_____

Were there any negative consequences to being honest? Yes / No

If Yes, how did that make you feel? _____

_____

What is the most important thing you learned from doing this dare? _____

_____

List 1 benefit that did or can result from confessing something you have already gotten away

with. _____

_____

CONGRATULATIONS ON YOUR SUCCESS

CHAPTER REVIEW

What is your favorite quote from this chapter? Why?

_____

_____

Which of the dares was the hardest? Why?

#_____ because _____

_____

_____

Which of the dares was the easiest? Why?

#_____ because _____

_____

_____

Which dare made you feel the best about what you had done? Why?

#_____ because _____

_____

_____

Which dare do you think you will try to do most often? Why?

#_____ because _____

_____

_____

Which dare did you do the most? #_____

Which dare did you do the least? #_____

Which dare was easiest to remember? #_____ hardest? #_____

Which dare had the most shocking/dramatic results? #_____ why? _____

_____

Which dare or dares did people seem to notice when you did it? _____

What did you learn about yourself and/or others through this chapter's exercises?

_____

_____

_____

_____

_____

_____

_____

Can you think of another way to dare yourself in order to test or build-up this virtue?

_____

_____

_____

_____

_____

_____

_____

_____

_____

What was fun about these exercises? _____

_____

_____

What was not so fun? _____

_____

Use these 2 pages to keep notes during the week, jot down ideas or thoughts, or to evaluate your success. Set goals to help you accomplish the dares and goals for practicing them in the future.

_____

_____

_____

_____

_____

_____

_____

_____

_____

_____

_____

_____

_____

_____

_____

_____

_____

_____

_____

_____

_____

_____

_____

_____

_____

_____

"It is not because things are difficult that we do not dare; it is because we do not dare that things are difficult."

~Seneca

"Honesty is the first chapter in the book of wisdom."

Thomas Jefferson

CHAPTER 2

RESPECT

Respect: a person's polite messages or attentions; treat with consideration; not offesive.

Disrespect: lack of respect; discourtesy.

As defined by *The Oxford illustrated Dictionary*

The Choice

Virtue: Respectful

or

Vice: Disrespectful

The greatest two benefits of being respectful are:

1.) _____

2.) _____

The two most detrimental consequences of being disrespectful are:

1.) _____

2.) _____

Respect Agreement

I, _____, understand that being respectful is more beneficial to me than being disrespectful. Therefore, I agree to read the following chapter, answer the questions presented, complete any exercises, and attempt to accomplish as many dares as possible - as often as I can.

Signed: _____   Date: _____

Dare 1

"We have two ears and one mouth so that we can listen twice as much as we speak."
~Epictetus, Greek philosopher

Dare to be respectful when communicating with others.

When communicating with others, there are two main things you can do to be respectful. The first would be to avoid dominating the conversation and interrupting or talking over people when they talk. Can you think of someone who habitually cuts others off when they are talking? How does it make you feel when someone speaks over you, interrupts you, or takes over the conversation while you are talking? If we assume that the person has no manners or just enjoys being rude, we may be willing and able to just blow it off or ignore them. However, when people seem to think that what they want to say is always more important than whatever we may have to say, we will likely be offended by their behavior. Out of anger or frustration, we might try talking louder than they are or just continue talking right over each other until someone finally gives up. Giving others the opportunity to finish their thoughts not only shows them respect, but it also minimizes the possibilities for misunderstandings and arguments. The second way to show respect can be a bit more difficult because it requires us to actually pay attention to what someone is saying. Do you ever find yourself thinking about your response before someone has even finished talking? While you are thinking about what you want to say, you may be missing important information that is still being directed towards you. **When you start thinking, you stop listening!** This is how simple conversations can turn into misunderstandings or heated arguments. Typically, one person will say, "Did you even listen to what I said?" or "I just said that, but you obviously weren't listening." Unfortunately, parents often think that their children aren't listening to them; while children are thinking that their parents are the ones who aren't listening. Most likely, they are both right! Truth is, good communication is a key ingredient for creating and maintaining healthy, long-lasting relationships. By being respectful within conversations, you not only show yourself to be a respectful person, but you also increase the effectiveness of your communications with others.

To accomplish this dare: Go a whole day without dominating conversations, interrupting or talking over others, and really listen to what they are saying. This may be more difficult than you think so here are a few sentences you can use to correct yourself if you slip up. "Excuse me, I am sorry I interrupted...Please continue," or "I am sorry, I got caught up in my own thinking. Could you please repeat that so I can understand your point?"

Be Aware: Listening is much more difficult than speaking. You might even get frustrated by how little time you will find to speak if you are being respectful. Then, when you do take an opportunity to speak, you may get cut off! This too may be very frustrating. Try not to take it personal. A great response would be, "Excuse me, please let me finish my point, and I will happily listen to yours."

Why do you think people so often speak over or interrupt one another? _____

_____

_____

Do you sometimes speak over or interrupt others? Yes / No If Yes, why do you think you

do that? _____

How do you feel when someone cuts you off, speaks over you, or interrupts you when you

are talking? _____ Why? _____

_____

Name one person who you think is in the habit of interrupting others, dominating

conversations, or doesn't pay attention when being spoken to. _____

Do you enjoy this person's company? Yes / Sometimes / Not usually / No

List one negative consequence that can result from habitually dominating conversations

and talking over or interrupting others? _____

_____

I (always / often / sometimes / rarely / never) miss what people are saying because I have
either stopped paying attention or started thinking of how I want to respond.

It is (very important / somewhat important / not important to me at all) that others listen
to me when I am speaking.

What will be the most difficult part of doing this dare? _____

In your opinion, what are the biggest benefits of being respectful within conversation?

_____

_____

Food for Thought: There may be times when you really feel as though you have to interrupt
someone, but you don't want to be disrespectful. In these cases, the way to best show respect
is to acknowledge you are interrupting and apologize for having to do so. Example: "I am
really sorry to interrupt you while you are talking but…."

Dare 2

"Wicked men obey from fear; good men, from love."   ~Aristotle

Dare to avoid putting off or complaining about your responsibilities.

Has complaining ever gotten you out of having to do what you are told? Does making parents or teachers tell you more than once ever make them forget they told you? Complaining about having to do something or putting off doing things we have to do doesn't make them any easier and often causes adults to feel disrespected and unappreciated. Truth is, sometimes we have to do things we don't want to do! Consider the responsibilities of most parents on a regular or even daily basis. They go to work, cook meals, clean toilets, fold clothes, wash dishes, pay bills, take out the trash, clean the floors, go to the grocery, and help with children's homework. Does any of that sound like fun to you? Just because parents don't put off or complain every day about the things they have to do doesn't mean that they want to do them! Sure, maybe sometimes they complain or remind you of all the responsibilities they have and all the things they do for you when they are feeling unappreciated or disrespected. However, most adults have learned that it doesn't help to complain or procrastinate when it comes to their responsibilities. When we consider the reasons why we have to do the things we don't want to do, we often realize that it makes more sense to appreciate the responsibility than it does to complain about it. For example, if your mom tells you to empty the dishwasher, ask yourself "why do I have to empty the dishwasher?" The answer is because you probably ate a nice hot meal for dinner on a clean plate and enjoyed a cold soda from a clean glass. Being thankful for those experiences should keep us from complaining about the resulting chore. To avoid putting chores off, consider how much harder they may be if you wait until later to get it done. For example, taking out the trash is always more difficult if you wait until the trash is overflowing all over the floor. If that doesn't provide you with enough motivation, remember: avoiding complaining about or putting off your responsibilities not only makes your parents feel respected and appreciated but it can also keep you from getting in trouble.

To accomplish this dare: Make it through 3 days without complaining about or putting off your responsibilities. Accomplishing the dare by not complaining is quite easy because really you are just being obedient. By taking the time to ask yourself why, you may learn to appreciate the responsibility and then you will do it out of love.

Be Aware: We may not always like the reasons we have to do certain things, but it is always beneficial to at least know what they are. If you can't think of a good reason why you have to do something, ask politely! Ex. "Mom, what benefit is there to cleaning my room?" If she doesn't think you are being sarcastic, she might say "A clutter and dust free room provides a safe and healthy environment to live in and makes things easier to find."

I am more likely to (complain about / put off doing) my chores/responsibilities.

One thing I tend to complain about having to do is _____

_____ because _____

What is one good reason why the chore/responsibility should be done? _____

_____

When I am complaining about having to do something, it takes (less time / more time / about the same amount of time) to get it done.

When I put off chores/responsibilities until later, they usually are (easier / harder) to do.

How do you think parents/teachers feel when they have to ask you more than once to do something or hear you complaining about what they have asked and/or need you to do?

_____

_____ Is this how you intended or wanted them to feel? Yes / No

How do you suppose a parent/teacher/adult would feel or respond if you did what they asked when they asked and without complaining? _____

_____

How would it make you feel? _____

Here are 4 benefits of being respectful. Number them 1 to 4, according to which you believe to be most beneficial. In your opinion, "1" would be the greatest benefit.

_____ I avoid getting in trouble, punished, or yelled at.

_____ The parent/teacher/adult feels respected and appreciated.

_____ The chore/responsibility gets done faster and I can return to what I want to be doing.

_____ I acknowledge and appreciate the things that lead to the chore/responsibility.

Food for Thought: It may be hard to believe, but many of the chores and responsibilities we have are a direct result of the things we love most. Here a few examples:

Eating well (cause) ➔ Doing dishes (chore)

Clean Clothes (cause) ➔ Folding Clothes (chore)

Having a pet (cause) ➔ Walking dog or emptying litter box (chore)

Having a yard to play in (cause) ➔ Mowing the lawn (chore)

Being healthy (cause) ➔ Dusting and vacuuming the house (chore)

Dare 3

"How much trouble he avoids who does not look to see what his neighbor says, does, or thinks."
~ Marcus Aurelius, Great Roman Emperor

Dare to respect the privacy of others.

People in general can be pretty nosey. How would you feel if your mother were going through everything in your room while you were at school or if you caught your father listening in on a very personal phone conversation? Most people feel betrayed, violated, angry, or hurt when someone disrespects or invades their privacy. However, sometimes the things people do that cause us to feel that way are actually things we have no problem doing to someone else. Truth is, even though personal privacy is usually important to everyone, it is rarely respected by anyone. Here are some common examples of how we can disrespect or invade someone's privacy.

1.) Eaves dropping in on conversations you are not invited to,
2.) Looking through someone's phone to see who they are calling or texting,
3.) Reading people's e-mails or searching through personal folders on their computer,
4.) Entering someone's room or home without knocking,
5.) Spreading rumors about people that can harm their reputation,
6.) Sharing anything told to you in confidence that you agreed to keep a secret,
7.) Repeating something you know someone else wouldn't want others to know.
8.) Going through someone's personal belongings, locker, closet, or furniture,
9.) Pressuring people for information that they are not openly or willingly sharing,
10.) Spying on or following people around without their knowledge.

Privacy is a lot like respect, wanting it is normal but giving it to others is not so easy.

To accomplish this dare: For 5 days, focus on respecting the privacy of others and successfully accomplish each of the following: 1.) Acknowledge when you are just about to or have already begun to invade someone's privacy and STOP! 2.) When you have an urge to or feel a desire to invade someone's privacy – DON'T. 3.) When you do (and you will) invade other's privacy… consider how you would feel if someone did the same thing to you and then apologize to the person you disrespected.

Be Aware: By putting your attention on respecting other's privacy, you are likely to see more attempts from others to invade your privacy. People will not actually be attempting to invade your privacy any more than usual, but because your attention is on respecting people's privacy you will be more aware of what is threatening your own. You can use these opportunities to encourage others to be more respectful of people's privacy by politely telling them how or when they are invading or disrespecting your own.

How important is it to you for others to respect your privacy?   (Circle one)

(extremely important / pretty important / somewhat important / not very important at all)

On a scale of 1 – 10, with 1 being never nosey and 10 being extremely nosey…how nosey would you say you are? (Circle one)   1 2 3 4 5 6 7 8 9 10

Out of all your friends and family, who tends to disrespect your privacy the most and how?

Who? _____ How? _____

_____

Do you have a place that you consider "your space" and really want to keep private? (For example, your room, an e-mail account, your cell phone, a locker at school, a diary, or a hiding space where you keep things you don't want anyone to see.)   Yes / No

If so, how would you feel if someone were to invade that space? _____

_____

Below is a list of common ways people disrespect others by invading their privacy. Put them in order starting with number 1 being the one you do the most and would find difficult to avoid doing – and number 10 being the one you would do the least or wouldn't have trouble avoiding.

_____ Eaves dropping in on conversations you are not invited to,
_____ Looking through someone's phone to see who they are calling or texting,
_____ Reading people's e-mails or searching through personal folders on their computer,
_____ Entering someone's room or home without knocking,
_____ Spreading rumors about people that can harm their reputation,
_____ Sharing anything told to you in confidence that you agreed to keep a secret,
_____ Repeating something you know someone else wouldn't want others to know.
_____ Going through someone's personal belongings, locker, closet, or furniture,
_____ Pressuring people for information that they are not openly or willingly sharing,
_____ Spying on or following people around without their knowledge.

From the list above, _____ would cause the most negative feelings for me or would be the last thing I would want someone to do to me.

Can you remember a time when you did that to someone else? Yes / No

From the list above, _____ would be the one that is most often done to me.

I have done (all / most / some / a few / none) of the things listed above to others.

31

Dare 4

"An animal will always look for a person's intention by looking them right in the eyes."

~H. Powers

Dare to have good eye contact when communicating with others.

At a very young age, you probably learned that looking away from what you were doing, even for a split second, could cause you to spill milk all over the counter or get hit in the face by a ball. Getting distracted or trying to split your attention among too many things usually ends up with someone yelling, "Look where you're going," or "Watch what you're doing." For the most part, when our eyes leave – our attention follows; if our attention leaves – our eyes follow. For instance, if you are watching TV in your room, and someone suddenly opens your door, your attention immediately shifts towards the door and your eyes will naturally follow. Even though people can't be certain of what our intentions are just by looking in our eyes, they can often tell where our attention is by observing what our eyes are doing. When it comes to communicating with others, good eye contact is often believed to be a sign of respect for the other person. However, there are many people who find it extremely difficult at times to look directly into the eyes of someone they respect. When you are lying, feelings of guilt or shame will often cause you to look away from the person you are talking to. If you're intimidated by or have strong emotions for someone you respect, feelings of unworthiness or embarrassment may cause you to spend more time talking to their feet than you do to their face. Keeping good eye contact with someone you respect can also be tough if you are not interested in the topic of the conversation or if you have something more important on your mind. Truth is, good eye contact is more about _giving respect to others_ than it is about _having respect for others_; it's an **act** of respect… not a **sign** of respect. Maintaining good eye contact during conversations allows us to focus our attention on what's being communicated both verbally and physically. Even though it is sometimes difficult to do, looking at the person you are talking to can really help you to listen better and communicate more effectively.

To accomplish this dare: For 1 whole day, be respectful to others by giving them your undivided attention within conversations. This does not mean you have to stare at them the whole time! That will likely make both of you uncomfortable. Just make as much eye contact as you feel comfortable doing and try not to get distracted by your surroundings.

Be Aware: Our eyes often say what our lips don't! Eye contact is a non-verbal form of communication that often reveals more of the Truth than our words do. Without uttering a word, people can frequently tell if we are mad, happy, embarrassed, sad, confused, angry, shocked, distracted, or even lost in thought. This is probably the main reason why people try to avoid making eye contact. However, no matter how hard you try, your eyes won't hide what is going on inside.

I think it is (important / not important) to look at people when in conversation with them.

I find it (very hard / somewhat difficult / easy / very easy) to look people in the eyes.

When I am talking, I am (comfortable / uncomfortable) if the person is looking at me.

I mostly (look away / look back and forth / look only at the person) during conversations.

(Very few / Some / Most) people have good eye contact when communicating with me.

Do you agree that having good eye contact can increase your attentiveness? Yes / No

Why? _____

Winking is a non-verbal form of communicating something with your eyes. List 2 things you might assume if someone winked at you. _____

_____

What might you assume if someone rolled their eyes at something you said? _____

_____

Put a check in front of all the statements that are true for you or that you would agree might cause you to look away while having a conversation.

____ I don't know the person   ____ I really "like" the person   ____ I don't like them

____ Person is intimidating   ____ I am distracted   ____ Person is crying

____ Person is yelling at me   ____ I disagree or doubt them   ____ I am lying

____ Topic is not interesting   ____ I am trying to hide my feelings

Food for Thought: There are many sensible reasons why some people struggle with making or keeping eye contact within different situations or with different people. The important thing is to identify what is the source/cause of these reasons. From the list above, there are 2 main sources creating the reasons which commonly reduce eye contact. The first and most obvious source is having an uncomfortable feeling. Whether you don't know the person, are intimidated by someone, are being yelled at, or don't know what to say to someone who is crying...you are very likely to be uncomfortable and looking away is your response to that feeling. The second source would be your level of attention. When you don't like a person, don't believe them, disagree with what they are saying, have other things on your mind, or don't care...your focus will not be on them because you're not willing to give them your attention.

RESPECT
Dare 5

"One of the greatest victories you can gain over someone is to beat him at politeness"

~Josh Billings, humor writer

Dare to be respectful by using polite language creatively.

One way parents teach their children to respect others, especially adults, is through the use of polite language. They teach their children to use words like please, thank you, yes sir, no ma'am, and excuse me whenever it's appropriate. Some parents will require their children to use polite language regularly. These children create a habit of using these words at a young age and will usually continue using polite language even as an adult. Other children will be exposed to polite language but may not be forced or required to use it. These children will be less likely to create a steady habit of showing others respect through the use of polite language. Is a child who uses polite language better than a child who does not? No. The difference in the usage of polite language is the result of what a child is taught and what expectations have been placed on them. You can be polite and not use polite language just as easily as you can use polite language in a not so polite way. Truth is, using polite language exemplifies good manners and can be learned at any stage in life. Most commonly, polite language is used as a very simple response or as a request. Thank you is used when someone gives you something, excuse me is used when you accidentally bump someone or when you burp, and please is used when you want something. However, polite language does not need to be limited to these specific or typical responses. Being creative with these words can make being respectful actually fun and may even make more of an impression on others than you think they would. Here are a few examples of how to use polite language - creatively.

"I am fine. **Thank You for asking**." - instead of just saying "fine" when asked "how are you?"
"I am not going to be able to do that; **Thanks for Understanding**." - instead of just saying "no"
"I am sorry I took so long; **Thank You for your patience**."
"**Excuse me**, I didn't hear you. Could you repeat that?" - instead of "What?" or "huh?"
"**Excuse me**, I don't mean to cut you off, but..." - instead of rudely interjecting or interrupting.
"**Excuse me**, may I help you with that?" - instead of just watching someone struggle.
"**Please**, be my guest!" - when someone asks to borrow something-instead of "Sure" or "Here"
"**Please**, let me get that for you." - as you open the door for someone or help pick up something.
"**Please do**, I would like that." - when someone asks if they can call you or join you at the table.
"**Yes ma'am,** I sure did." - if your mom asks you if you did your homework - instead of "Yep!"
"**No sir,** I haven't yet." - when your dad asks if you took out the trash - instead of "I'm gonna!"

To accomplish this dare: For 3 consecutive days, use polite language as often as possible and in front of as many people as you can - especially your parents, teachers, friends and siblings! See if they notice! Be creative - try to use at least 5 sentences from above and make up one of your own. Also, use ma'am and sir when addressing or answering adults.

As a young child, were you **exposed** to polite language?   Yes / No

Were you **required** to use polite language growing up?   Yes / No

How do you feel when you are using polite language? _____

_____

Do you use polite language or act more respectful for someone in particular? Yes / No

If yes, who is it and why? _____

I think polite language is used by (the majority of / the minority of / not enough) people.

Do you find that polite language is used by specific groups of people? Yes / No

If Yes, what groups would they be? Example: Rich? Religious? Elderly? _____

Create at least one creative sentence using either "Thank You," "Excuse me," "Pardon me," or "Please."

_____

_____

Of all the people you know, who uses polite language the most? _____

(Consider asking them what are some of the benefits they get from using polite language.)

Do you think anyone will notice when you are doing this dare? Yes / No If yes, who do

you think will notice and what response would you expect? _____

_____

I think it would be (very hard / somewhat hard / not too hard / very easy) for me to learn and use creative polite language regularly.

Food for Thought: If you already have a steady habit of being respectful to adults by using polite language, this dare may be somewhat easy for you. Try to challenge yourself to find more creative ways to use your words and practice being consistent by using polite language no matter who you are talking to. If you are not in the habit of using polite language regularly, this dare may be a bit more difficult than you think. It may even feel like you are trying to learn a foreign language. Just try to use the words as often as possible and remember that learning something new takes time, practice, and commitment.

Dare 6

"Thank God men cannot fly, and lay waste the sky as well as the Earth."

~Henry David Thoreau

Dare to respect the environment and other people's property.

Have you ever thrown trash out a car window or stuck a piece of gum somewhere it didn't belong? When you pretend your trash is a basketball but completely miss the shot, do you go back and pick it up or do you leave it there for someone else to rebound? Typically, what we decide to do with our trash will depend on whether or not someone is watching us. The same is true when it comes to being destructive or vandalizing someone else's property. People don't throw rocks through windows or spray paint a wall without first checking to see if the 'coast is clear.' When it comes to respecting the environment and other people's property, avoiding being seen or getting caught seems to be the only thing that matters. Truth is, most people feel uncomfortable littering and being destructive even when no one sees them or if they escape without getting caught. This uncomfortable feeling often comes from knowing what we ought to do, but choosing not to do it. Sometimes, our own personal experiences are what create these uncomfortable feelings. Imagine you are walking through a parking lot and you suddenly step on a huge pile of sticky, pink gum with your brand new shoes. You will probably get very angry, and you may even say something like "Only a complete jerk would spit their gum out in the middle of a parking lot for someone to step on when there is a garbage can just 5 feet away!" Even if you have done the same thing in the past, this experience may keep you from ever doing it again. By taking a moment to consider how we would feel about someone doing to us, or our personal property, what we are about to do... we force ourselves to acknowledge our choice to be disrespectful and accept living with the guilt that often comes with it.

To accomplish this dare: There are 3 ways to accomplish this dare. You can choose to avoiding littering and vandalizing for any entire week. The more courageous people will make a commitment to pick up any trash they may see lying around. Yep, that's right... the trash you didn't put there. For 3 days, anytime you see trash, you would have to pick it up. Picking up behind people who are disrespectful to their environment can help you to develop an appreciation for cleanliness. Or, an extremely daring person may offer to paint a wall that has been vandalized with graffiti within their community or help clean up around their school. Always get permission to do these types of public service from parents, teachers, or local officials.

Be Aware: You can't get credit for this dare if you have vandalized or destroyed any public property at school or around your neighborhood any time after reading this chapter. That means... no writing or graffiti on desks, lockers, bathroom stalls, stop signs, walls, or even your own furniture. You can't have stuck your gum anywhere it shouldn't be and you can't use eggs or toilet paper to decorate anyone's car or house.

I will accomplish this dare by:

    1.) simply avoiding littering and respecting public property for an entire week,

    2.) attempting to pick up litter and clean up around school/neighborhood for 3 days,

    3.) being actively involved in 1 activity that helps to clean up the environment or my community.

Are you typically someone who litters or disrespects public property? Yes / No

I am (always / sometimes / never) tempted to put gum where it doesn't belong, throw trash out a window or leave my trash on the ground.

Have you ever destroyed, damaged, or vandalized property that didn't belong to you?

Yes / No If Yes, what did you do and why? _____

_____

Did you feel guilty for this action? Yes / No

How do you feel when someone is destructive or irresponsible with your personal things?

_____

What was the worst experience that you or your family had to endure as a result of someone

disrespecting or vandalizing your property? _____

_____

How did that experience make you feel? _____

_____

List 2 things people do which disrespects the environment or other people's property that

irritate you. _____

_____

What do you appreciate the most about the environment you live in? _____

_____

How does being in a dirty environment make you feel? _____

ACCOMPLISHED
Respect Dare 1

I found it (very hard / hard / not too hard / very easy) to go a whole day without interrupting others.

I found that (adults / teenagers / younger children) interrupt me the most.

I seem to interrupt (adults / my friends / younger children) the most.

Did you catch yourself thinking of responses while the other person was still talking? Yes / No

Did being respectful make it harder to find an opportunity to speak? Yes / No

If Yes, how did that make you feel? _____

_____

Did you use the statements "Excuse me, I am sorry I interrupted, Please continue." or "I am sorry, I wasn't listening. Could you please repeat that?"

Yes / No If Yes, about how many times? _____

How did using the suggested statements make you feel? _____

_____

The most important thing I learned from doing this dare was _____

_____

For me to create a habit of always letting others complete their thoughts and sentences without interrupting them would take (a lot / some / just a little of) practice.

CONGRATULATIONS ON YOUR SUCCESS

ACCOMPLISHED
Respect Dare 2

Accomplishing the dare was (harder than I thought / easy / nearly impossible)

I complain and procrastinate (too much / sometimes / rarely).

I found it harder to avoid (complaining / procrastinating).

When I did what I was asked without complaining or procrastinating I felt

(proud of myself / like I deserved a reward / like complaining the whole time)

Did acknowledging '**why**' you have to do a chore/responsibility lessen your desire to complain about it?   Yes / No

When I am asked or told do something that I **don't** want to do, I usually

(do it right away / do it when I am finished what I am currently doing / do it when I feel like it / get in trouble for not doing it)

In a normal situation, how many times does a parent have to ask you to do something before you do it? (once / twice / three times / more than they should)

The biggest disadvantage of complaining and procrastinating is _____

_____

How hard do you think it would be for you to create the habit of showing parents, teachers and other adults respect by avoiding complaining and procrastinating?

(extremely hard / somewhat hard / not too hard / not hard at all)

Knowing the benefits of respect, how hard will you try to create this habit?

1	2	3	4	5	6	7	8	9	10

<not too hard>   <hard>   <very hard>

CONGRATULATIONS ON YOUR SUCCESS

Respect Dare 3

Accomplishing this dare was (harder / easier) than I expected.

I respect other's privacy (most of the time / sometimes / hardly ever).

The time I was most tempted to disrespect someone's privacy was when _____
_____
_____

The reason I think it was hard for me was because _____
_____

In trying to respect other's privacy, I learned that I struggle the most with

    1.) _____

    2.) _____

When it comes to my privacy, the thing that people do that bothers me the most is _____
_____

In order to be a little more respectful of other's privacy, I will need to practice _____
_____

I am glad I did this dare because _____

The most important thing I learned from or want to remember about this dare is _____
_____

Will you continue to practice respecting others privacy?   Yes / No

CONGRATULATIONS ON YOUR SUCCESS

Respect Dare 4

Accomplishing this dare was: (very difficult / somewhat difficult / more difficult than I thought it would be / somewhat easy / very easy)

The most important thing I learned from doing this dare was _____

_____

_____

For me, the most common reason or **source** for looking away during conversations would

be _____

Do you think that this source is the **most common** for people who struggle making eye contact?   Yes / No / Not sure

When you look at the person talking, is your level of attentiveness higher?   Yes / No

Has this dare made you more aware of where you look during conversations?   Yes / No

How likely are you to continue to do this dare?

(Not likely / Not as likely as I would like to be / Somewhat likely / Very likely)

What can you do to be more comfortable with making eye contact with others or how could

you encourage others who struggle? _____

_____

What is the greatest benefit of good eye contact? _____

_____

CONGRATULATIONS ON YOUR SUCCESS

Respect Dare 5

Accomplished this dare was (very difficult / somewhat difficult / more difficult than I thought it would be / somewhat easy / very easy)

I was (a lot / somewhat / not much) more respectful than I usually am.

During the 3 days, I believe I used (plenty / a lot / some / a little) of creative polite language and I am (proud of / OK with / disappointed about) that.

Being more respectful and using polite language creatively made me feel _____

_____

When you accomplished the dare, did anyone notice you using polite language creatively or being respectful? Yes / No

If Yes, what was their reaction? _____

_____

My favorite creative sentence using polite language was _____

_____

Do you intend to practice using polite language more often?   Yes / No

If No, why? _____

Consider and list 2 benefits of using polite language.

    1.) _____

    2.) _____

The most important thing I want to remember about being respectful by using polite language

is _____

TRUTH AND DARE

CONGRATULATIONS ON YOUR SUCCESS

Respect Dare 6

I accomplished this dare by _____

_____

The hardest part of this dare was _____

_____

Accomplishing this dare made me feel _____

The amount of littering and vandalism in my school and community is

(less than / more than) I expected it to be.

Did doing this dare make you more aware of the littering and vandalizing that goes on or exists within your community or school?   Yes / No

Did you witness any littering or vandalism while you were focused on accomplishing this dare? Yes / No If Yes, how did it make you feel?

_____

One thing I learned from doing this dare is _____

_____

Do you intend to continue practicing respect the environment? Yes / No

_____ I avoided vandalizing and was not destructive of public property at any time since reading this dare. (Remember, this must be checked to have accomplished this dare. If you have been destructive of public property, you must repair the damage or at least confess it to an adult. Then return to complete dare.)

CONGRATULATIONS ON YOUR SUCCESS

CHAPTER REVIEW

What is your favorite quote from this chapter? Why?

_____

_____

Which of the dares was the hardest? Why?

_____ because _____

_____

_____

Which of the dares was the easiest? Why?

_____ because _____

_____

_____

Which dare made you feel the best about what you had done? Why?

_____ because _____

_____

_____

Which dare do you think you will try to do most often? Why?

_____ because _____

_____

_____

Which dare did you do the most? #_____

Which dare did you do the least? #_____

Which dare was easiest to remember? #_____ hardest? #_____

Which dare had the most shocking/dramatic results? #_____ why? _____

_____

Which dare or dares did people seem to notice when you did it? _____

What did you learn about yourself and/or others through this chapter's exercises?

_____

_____

_____

_____

_____

_____

_____

Can you think of another way to dare yourself in order to test or build-up this virtue?

_____

_____

_____

_____

_____

_____

_____

_____

_____

What was fun about these exercises? _____

_____

_____

What was not so fun? _____

_____

Use these 2 pages to keep notes during the week, jot down ideas or thoughts, or to evaluate your success. Set goals to help you accomplish the dares and goals for practicing them in the future.

_____

_____

_____

_____

_____

_____

_____

_____

_____

_____

_____

_____

_____

_____

_____

_____

_____

_____

_____

_____

_____

_____

_____

_____

_____

_____

_____

_____

_____

"It is not because things are difficult that we do not dare; it is because we do not dare that things are difficult."
~Seneca

"Without feelings of respect,
what is there to distinguish men from beast?"

Confucius

CHAPTER 3

GENEROSITY

Generous: giving willingly and freely; (True generosity, is giving for, and wanting only to receive, the joy of giving. There is no need to be acknowledge or appreciated. As a result, being **willing** to give is much easier than **freely** giving.)

Greedy: having or showing an excessive desire or need for excess (more).

As defined by *The Oxford illustrated Dictionary*

The Choice

Virtue: Generosity

or

Vice: Greediness

The greatest two benefits of being generosity are:

1.) _____

2.) _____

The two most detrimental consequences of being greedy are:

1.) _____

2.) _____

Generosity Agreement

I, _____, understand that being generous is more beneficial to me than being greedy. Therefore, I agree to read the following chapter, answer the questions presented, complete any exercises, and attempt to accomplish as many dares as possible – as often as I can.

Signed: _____   Date: _____

Dare 1

"**Real generosity is doing something nice for someone who will never find out it was from you.**"

~Frank A. Clark

Dare to give a gift to someone without letting anyone know it's from you.

Not all 'secret admirers' have to be romantic ones, nor does it have to be a special occasion to give someone a gift or a friendly encouraging note. Imagine how you would feel if you arrive at your desk and found your favorite candy with a note of encouragement beside it. The note isn't signed and no one confesses to giving it to you. At first, not knowing who gave you the candy will probably drive you crazy. You may be more focused on finding out who it's from than you are about how receiving it makes you feel. Eventually, if you don't find out who did it, just knowing that someone was thinking about you and wanted to give you a gift will likely be enough to make you very happy. Truth is, being admired, acknowledged, or appreciated by others can really make us feel good about who we are. Deep down, we all want to be special to someone or at least want to feel like we matter to the people in our lives. Even if we know that we are special to someone, we still love (and sometimes even need) to hear or see an expression of their feelings for us. Unfortunately, people often wait for holidays to express how they feel about one another and birthdays end up being the only day of the year that we really feel special or important at all. Giving an anonymous gift to someone can make them feel like it's their birthday no matter what day it is.

To accomplish this dare: Give someone an anonymous gift or encouraging note to let them know that they are being thought of or appreciated. You can sneak a flower on a teacher's desk, leave a candy bar for a friend, encourage someone who appears to be down or sad with an anonymous note, or leave a toy you don't use on the porch of a neighbor who has a child who would love to play with it. Although you only need to record one event to accomplish this dare, challenge yourself to do it 3 times and record the one that you enjoyed the most. Remember, staying anonymous is the key to this dare. Telling just one person allows you to be acknowledged – and the dare remains incomplete. Also, pay attention to others when they are being generous and try to notice whether or not they seek to be acknowledged and appreciated for what they did. You will likely find that others are quick to tell people all the wonderful things they do that show off their generosity!

Be Aware: As stated in the introduction of this chapter, being willing to give is easier than giving freely. This dare is designed to help you understand the truth of that claim by letting you experience what it feels like to give freely and allowing you to feel the joy that true generosity brings. If the dare is done correctly, you will feel as though you, too, were given a gift.

Use "N" for never, "R" for rarely, "S" for sometimes, "O" for often, or "A" for always to identify how you really feel about giving both willingly and freely.

I _____ want to be thanked for the things I give to others.

I _____ expect to be acknowledge and appreciated when I do something for someone.

I _____ regret what I do for others when they don't seem to appreciate it.

I _____ feel taken advantage of by others when I am generous.

I _____ give things to others or do favors for people because I want to get their approval.

(Giving willingly / Giving freely) seems to be harder for me. Why? _____

_____

_____

How do you think you would feel if someone accomplished this dare on you? Why?

_____

_____

What are your initial thoughts about how you want to accomplish this dare? _____

_____

Giving anonymously eliminates any chance of being acknowledged and appreciated by others. How does this make you feel and how does it affect your willingness to give?

_____

_____

_____

Do you know someone who gives willingly and freely? Yes / No If Yes, who is it and what makes you think this about them? _____

_____

Food for Thought: Giving freely means never using "Remember when I did this for you" as a bargaining chip to get what you want. It also means you can't think it either. If you are thinking, "Just yesterday I gave that person money for lunch and today they are talking poorly about me to others," then you didn't give freely. You expected respect and loyalty for your generosity. Giving freely means not keeping an inventory of your generosity. You give, then forget — so never to regret.

Dare 2

"To do more for the world than the world does for you – that is success."

~Henry Ford

Dare to give away the things you don't use or need anymore.

At a very young age, we are taught to take care of the things that are important to us. Your parents may have said, "You better pick up your toys and put them where they belong or you might lose them." Even if you rarely ever listened, you probably jumped up right away if it was something you had a special bond with or you had a strong attachment to. Some things were just too important to lose or let go of. However, the things that were once a "must have" eventually become not so important. Toys, clothes, collectible cards, and books often go out of style long before they are all used up. At 8 years old, you just had to have the entire set of Pokemon cards or Barbie doll shoes. Now, you wouldn't dare to be seen playing with them or even having them. So they sit in the back of your closet with your clothes that are too small and the books you have read only once, if ever at all. Why do you think it is so hard to part with some of these things? Maybe you are just being lazy or don't feel like going through them. Perhaps you have physically outgrown certain things but want to keep them for emotional reasons. Truth is, sometimes giving something useless away can feel just like losing something of value. We live in a society which believes 'the more you have… the better you are.' The thought, 'If I am giving something away I must be losing something' convinces us that it is better to have than it is to give. So, we hold on to things we don't need or want anymore even though we know that they may be of great value to someone else. Yet, if someone cleaned out your closet and gave away the things you didn't want or need anymore, you probably wouldn't even notice or care that they were gone! Doing it yourself allows you to feel the joy of being generous!

To accomplish this dare: Get permission from your parents to clean out your closet, room, and dresser drawers. That shouldn't be hard to do! As you are going through your toys and things, use this simple rule: If you don't use it…lose it. When it comes to your clothes, use: If you don't wear it…share it. You could donate your toys and books to a local children's hospital, children's charity, or perhaps someone you know who would really enjoy them. The Salvation Army, Red Cross or a GoodWill store would be a great place to bring the clothes you have outgrown or games that you don't want anymore.

Be Aware: When you clean out your closet and get rid of the things you don't wear, want or use anymore, you may find yourself wanting to go shopping the next day to replace what you think you have lost. Try to remember that your Self-worth comes from Who You Are and not from the amount of physical things you possess. The only things worth having are the things you use, value and appreciate. Everything else is just clutter, and a cluttered home leads to a cluttered mind.

In my honest opinion, I have (way too many / a lot of / just enough / very few) clothes.

In my honest opinion, I have (way too many / a lot of / just enough / very few) things.

I will probably find (plenty of / some / just a few) items I am willing to give away.

I seem to (hold on to / let go of) belongings after I am done with them.

I would have to say that I (do / do not) have attachments to my belongings.

Of all my belongings, the one that I seem most attached to is _____.

What is your initial feeling about giving away things that you don't need, fit, want or use
anymore? _____

_____

What item, if any, do you think you might have trouble parting with? _____

Why? _____

Who might be appreciative of having the items you intend to give away? _____

How do you think you will feel when you give these items away? _____

_____

Some people love to hold onto everything and are often called junk collectors. Who do you
know that is like this and why do you think they like to hold on to all their things?

_____

_____

Food for Thought: When going through your things, you may find that there are items you
would like to hold on to for sentimental reasons. This dare is not designed to judge yourself
as good, bad or greedy with regard to how much you have. The dare is designed to allow you
to experience the joy of giving and to remind you of how important it is to appreciate and
value what you do have. So don't get rid of anything that doesn't make you feel good about
giving it away. You will probably find that only a few items actually have that much personal
importance to you. The things you don't value much anymore will likely have value to others
if you dare to take the opportunity to give them away.

Dare 3

"We make a living by what we get, we make a life by what we give."

~ Sir Winston Churchill

Dare to give up something that you value or want.

It's late at night and you are craving ice cream. When you get to the freezer, you notice there is only enough for one more bowl. Your mom was the only one who didn't get a bowl last night when the gallon was opened. Do you eat it without asking her if she wants it? Or do you take the chance of asking her, knowing she will probably want it? Being generous is easier when there is no feeling of loss attached to it. When giving up something means you will likely have to go without, another virtuous quality is often needed to motivate you into being generous. This other quality would be consideration. To be considerate means to be thoughtful of the needs, wants, rights, and feelings of others. Unfortunately, people are often more inconsiderate than they may like to think they are. This is because being inconsiderate is frequently not something we do deliberately or intentionally. Truth is, we just don't think about the wants, needs, rights, or feelings of others when it comes to having or getting the things we want. We just open the freezer, see the ice cream, and decide to eat it. Being considerate by regarding the wants, needs, rights, and feelings of others takes effort, a lot of practice, and a real commitment to being mindful of others. However, being inconsiderate isn't the only thing that keeps us from being generous. Greed can also block our motivation. When this happens, being generous feels more like a sacrifice than it does a joy. So, we choose to keep things for ourselves instead of sharing what we have with others.

To accomplish this dare: Share or give up something you have with someone who wants or needs it. Splitting a candy bar that you could easily finish alone, giving up your place in line to someone who seems to be in a hurry, or giving up your turn in a game so someone who hasn't played yet can get in are a few good ways to be generous. For the more daring teenager, the thing that is often the hardest to give up is your time. You have big plans for the weekend, but your parents need you to watch a younger sibling or want to include you in their plans. When what you want to do varies from what your parents want or need you to do, attempt to compromise…but if that fails…try being as considerate and generous as you can.

Be Aware: Remember, generosity requires a willingness to give freely. Giving up something you value or want **–willingly–** is difficult and can often feel like a sacrifice. This dare is not trying to teach you that sacrificing the things you desire or want for others is the right thing to do. If giving feels like a sacrifice, then your attention is focused on what you are losing rather than the joy of giving. In this case, giving will not make you feel good, may cause you to regret your decision, and can create a feeling of lack or loss. To prevent this, wait until being generous feels good or at least until your attention is on the joy of giving before you give away something you want or value.

On a scale of 1 – 10, with 1 being 'not at all' and 10 being 'extremely,' use a circle to show how generous you are and a square to show how considerate you are of others?

1   2   3   4   5   6   7   8   9   10

Do you find you are more generous with things you do **not** value or want? Yes / No

Mark each of the following statements as true or false.

_____   I am always willing to share or give up something I want if someone asks.

_____   If I want or value something, I should not have to give it away.

_____   When other people want something of mine, I usually give it to them.

_____   When I give away something I want or value to make someone else happy, I often feel like I have made a sacrifice.

_____   When I choose not to give up something when asked, I feel guilty about it.

_____   People have to ask me for something; I usually don't just give things away.

_____   Just because I give away something I want or value doesn't mean I have to see it as a sacrifice or loss.

_____   When deciding whether to give up something I want or value, I consider who wants it more.

Food for Thought: Did you think there was a right or wrong answer for the statements above? Perhaps you thought the first statement should be true. The word 'always' in that question was used to get you thinking of what the consequences of that may be. If you are always willing to give up what you want for someone else just because they asked…have you not cheated yourself? Did you struggle with how to answer the second statement? Maybe you wanted to say true but thought it would make you seem selfish or greedy. What about the third statement? Couldn't answering this true lead people to take advantage of your generosity? Furthermore, while answering the last statement true would seem like an honorable and reasonable thing to do, isn't it more important to appreciate and value the things we have rather than just wanting to have it? Truth is, these statements are just random statements used to examine what you think and how you feel about being generous. Each statement may be true or false and will often be answered differently based on the circumstances at the time and the people involved.

GENEROSITY
Dare 4

"When helping others, don't look for a reward; if you are looking for a reward, don't help others."

~Chinese Proverb

Dare to be generous with your time by doing something helpful for someone and refusing payment.

It may surprise you, but being helpful is often motivated by the hope for a reward. It may be a financial reward such as money that motivates someone to be helpful or perhaps a "feel good" reward such as being recognized or appreciated. Sometimes, we help people because we know it is the right thing to do but then expect that person to be just as willing when we ask for their help. Truth is, real generosity has no motives and needs or expects no reward. Being generous with your time means doing something helpful for no other reason than wanting and being able to help. If you cut someone's grass or wash their car for money, you may be helping them accomplish something they need done but this is not an act of generosity. Remember, generosity requires no return or payment. This does not mean that you need to give up your grass cutting business to be a generous person, but perhaps you can give them a free week once a year to show your customers how much you appreciate their business. By offering your assistance to people without fearing they will take you up on the offer, you will experience the joy of giving. You can create many opportunities to be helpful to others by asking, "May I help you with that?" or "What can I do to help you?"

To accomplish this dare: Be generous with your time by being helpful to someone and refusing any kind of payment. You could offer to help someone put their groceries in their car, tutor a student in school who may be struggling, bring someone's trashcan to or from the street on trash day, or wash your parent's car. Offering to help around the house with things that are not your chores also accomplishes this dare. However, a key element of this dare is to refuse a payment. A neighbor or someone in your community may be more likely to offer a payment than a parent would be. If you have made 3 attempts to accomplish this dare and have not been offered a financial reward, simply saying "No thanks necessary, I enjoyed being able to help" when they thank you will be enough to accomplish the dare.

Be Aware: Consider the things that motivate you. Money, success, recognition, and acceptance are often at the top of the list of things that motivate people into action. All are possible rewards for your labor and getting a job done. But what if you had been asked to consider the things that motivate you to do good or be helpful? Do you think money, success, recognition, and acceptance would still hold at the top of the list? Or would the feelings of being 'joyful to give' and 'happy to help' be better rewards?

What motivates you? Add your own, then number them 1 to 7 (1 = what motivates you most and 7 = what motivates you the least.)

(money/happiness/acknowledgment/success/other's approval/appreciation/ _____)

_____   _____   _____   _____   _____   _____   _____

When I help someone, I (never / sometimes / often) expect them to return the favor.

Which of the following would motivate you to help immediately, without being asked, and HAPPY to do so? Use "Y" for yes or "N" for no. Be honest and go with your first answer.

_____ A sibling is not feeling well but their daily chores have got to be done.

_____ A friend is stranded on the side of the road; their car ran out of gas.

_____ Someone you don't like just twisted their ankle and there is no one else around to help them up or take them to someone who can help.

_____ Your mom is doing the dishes from dinner even though she is feeling really sick.

_____ As you are getting out the car with your friends, the lady parked next to you drops all 4 of her bags of groceries; things are rolling everywhere.

_____ As you rush to get the trash can to the curb because the truck is coming, you notice that your neighbors trash is over-flowing but they haven't brought it to the curb.

_____ An elderly neighbor opens her door and her dog takes off running down the street.

_____ You go outside and see 3 very young girls struggling to get a bicycle chain back on and know that you would be able to fix it rather quickly.

_____ It just started to rain and you notice your neighbors car windows are down.

Would you expect or desire a financial reward for doing any of the above? Yes / No

When you don't stop to help, do you try to justify your decision or make excuses? Yes / No

When deciding whether to help, what is more important? (Who it is / How urgent it is)

Does the presence of others, especially your friends, influence your decision to help?

Yes / No If Yes, how so? _____

Have you ever wanted to help someone in need but chose not to or turned away? Yes / No

Have you ever wanted to help but the opportunity passed while you were deciding whether or not to act? Yes / No

Do you ever look to see if someone else will help first – so you won't have to? Yes / No

Dare 5

"People will forget what you said, will forget what you did, but they will not forget how you made them feel."

~Maya Angelou, poet

Dare to be generous with compliments and kind words.

Even if you don't think it is true, doesn't it feel great when someone gives you a compliment? How would you feel if someone you don't even know says "That is an awesome outfit," as they walk past you on the street? That outfit is likely to become your new favorite thing to wear for a while. Have you ever stopped to think about how powerful your words are? Giving compliments can be a very easy, fun, and effective way of developing or building up someone's self esteem. However, insults can also be easy to say and are just as effective at destroying someone's self esteem as compliments are at building it up. If someone you care about says "You don't look good in red," you might choose never to wear red again even if it's your favorite color. As odd as it is, people tend to believe the insults others say about them more often and readily than they do the compliments. As a result, there are more people suffering from low self esteem in the world than there are people who actually feel good about themselves or really love the person they are. Truth is, we often **think** a lot more *compliments* than we **give,** and we **speak** more *insults* than we would want to **take.** Shouldn't it be the other way around? Imagine how much better society could be or how good we would feel if people spoke more compliments than they took and thought more insults than they actually gave.

To accomplish this dare: For one whole day, try to compliment as many people as you can and refrain from insulting anyone. A compliment does not have to be something physical; like their clothes, hair, body, or looks. You can compliment people on their behaviors, attitudes, personality, or even a specific quality or talent they possess. Try to give an equal amount of physical and non-physical compliments. For the really daring person, try to say 2 compliments for every insult or negative comment that is said about anyone throughout the day. Imagine little (+) and (-) signs filling the air and try to get the positive comments spoken about others to outweigh the negative by the end of the day. This will certainly be a task!

Be Aware: If giving people compliments makes you feel nervous or uncomfortable, it will be helpful to learn the reason why before trying to accomplish this dare. When you see an old lady who has obviously taken her time to fix her hair and do her make-up, ask yourself "What is keeping me from telling her... You sure look pretty today?" People with low self esteem often struggle with giving and accepting compliments. Some people will even argue with you when you give them a compliment or try to convince you that what you said isn't true. You do not have to get others to agree with or accept your compliments in order to accomplish the dare. Just look for the good in people and when you see it – say it!

Do you typically give compliments frequently?   Yes / No

Do you take compliments well?   Yes / No

How do you feel when you are given a compliment? _____

_____

How do you feel when you are giving someone a compliment? _____

_____

Which are more commonly spoken amongst your friends? (insults / compliments)

How do you feel about complimenting people you don't know? _____

_____

I (often / sometimes / rarely) compliment my parents, teachers, or other adults.

I (often / sometimes / rarely) compliment younger children.

I (often / sometimes / rarely) take the opportunity to compliment myself.

Do you think you get more compliments or give more compliments? (get / give)

Do you ever think of a compliment but don't share it? Yes / No If Yes, why do you

think you keep it to yourself or what prevents you from sharing it? _____

_____

When I compliment others, it is more often a (physical / non-physical) quality.

When others compliment me, it is usually an (physical / non-physical) quality.

The most common compliment I get from others is _____

Food for Thought: Can you think of a person who you would **not** want to compliment because they already think too highly of themselves? Truth is, people who think highly of themselves don't usually feel a need to let others know it. Often, it is the people who act like they are special and seem overly confident who need the most reassurance. These people rarely get compliments from anyone other than themselves. Even though you may not like the response you will get, try to give a compliment to someone who you may think doesn't need it. Complimenting a friend is easy, but complimenting a stranger or even an enemy may gain you a new friend.

GENEROSITY
Dare 6

"Silent gratitude isn't much use to anyone."

~Gladys Bertha Stern, English Novelist

Dare to look for and acknowledge other's generosity.

People are often labeled as 'givers' or 'takers.' Givers are usually people who love being of service to others and enjoy being generous with their time or their belongings. As long as they are able to share and help others, they are very willing to do so. Takers often fail to recognize what people do for them and rarely do they appreciate the things they have. You can probably think of many times in which you did something for someone and felt as though they didn't appreciate or even notice how you helped them. Even though true generosity requires no rewards, it is normal for someone to feel unappreciated or taken for granted when the things they do for others go unnoticed. People can feel really great when they are being generous but may soon regret what they did if they don't get the response that they wanted or felt they deserved. Truth is, people who appear to be givers their whole lives often end up being very bitter towards the takers in their lives. However, when givers are acknowledged and appreciated regularly by the takers who benefit from their generosity, they are more likely to enjoy and remain being the giving person they have always been. Being acknowledged and appreciated makes them feel good about Who they Are and allows them to focus on the joy they experience when giving to and helping others. Expressing your gratitude for someone's generosity often allows others to benefit from yours!

To accomplish this dare: Look for people being generous and encourage at least 3 of them by acknowledging what they have given or done for others. If you witness someone sharing or sacrificing for someone else…you have witnessed a generous act. If you catch yourself thinking "He/She didn't have to do that," or "I can't believe they just gave that away," than you have a great opportunity to acknowledge someone's generosity. When you witness someone going out of their way to be kind or offering help instead of saying "That's not my job," you have been given an opportunity to acknowledge their generosity.

Be Aware: Though it often seems like givers never take and takers never give, labeling people as either one or the other is unfair to the individual. We are all capable of being both a giver and a taker even though we usually are better at being one more than the other. It is important to understand that they both have their advantages and their disadvantages. Givers love to give and help people so much that they sometimes struggle with receiving help or taking things from others. Takers can get so accustomed to receiving things or help from others that they forget to acknowledge or appreciate who is doing the giving. Takers frequently get what they want while givers usually have to settle for leftovers. For this reason, it is best to practice and enjoy both giving and receiving.

TRUTH AND DARE

What is the most generous act you have ever heard about or witnessed? _____

_____

What is the most generous thing you have done and what motivated you to do this?

_____

_____

How did the person respond and how important was their response to you? _____

_____

What are you most generous with? (money / time / kind words / personal belongings /

other _____)

Do you think people would label you as a giver or taker? _____

Why do you think that? _____

Who is one person that has been extremely generous towards you? _____

What did they do for you or give you? _____

_____

How has their generosity impacted your life? _____

_____

When you witness or hear about someone being generous, how often do you acknowledge
what they did or gave? (never / rarely / sometimes / often / always)

Have you ever felt unappreciated or taken for granted by someone? Yes / No

If Yes, what effect did that experience have on your willingness to be generous or on the

relationship? _____

What do you think people should be more generous with? Add your own, then number them
1 – 9 (1= most important for people to be generous with and 9 = least important)

money / time / support / acceptance / love / belongings / trust / compliments / _____

_____   _____   _____   _____   _____   _____   _____   _____   _____

ACCOMPLISHED
Generosity Dare 1

Who did you pick to accomplish this dare on? _____

Why? _____

What did you do to accomplish this dare? _____

_____

_____

What thoughts or feelings did you have when doing this dare? _____

_____

Were you able to see or hear how the person responded? Yes / No If Yes, what was their

response? _____

Were you tempted to tell someone? Yes / No If Yes, why do you think you wanted to tell?

_____

Did you ever give in to your desire to tell someone and then have to do the dare again?

Yes / No If Yes, how many times? _____

I noticed that others are (very likely / somewhat likely / not likely at all) to talk about what they have done for, or have given to, others.

I would like to accomplish this dare (daily / weekly / monthly / never again).

The most important thing I learned from doing this dare was _____

_____

CONGRATULATIONS ON YOUR SUCCESS

Generosity Dare 2

I accomplished this dare by giving away _____

_____ to _____.

How did you feel doing this dare? _____

When going through your things, did you recall how you felt when you got them or consider how important they were to you? Yes / No

Was there an item that was hard to part with? Yes / No

Were there any items you were unable to part with? Yes / No

If Yes, what was it and why couldn't you part from it? _____

_____

After giving away my things, I (put a check before statements that are true)

      _____ wanted to give away more.

      _____ appreciated what I still had more.

      _____ wanted to get new things to replace them.

      _____ had a feeling of loss.

      _____ didn't feel like I lost anything of value.

      _____ acknowledged how much I take for granted the things I have.

      _____ saw the importance of giving away items I wasn't using or needed anymore.

What are some items that you really value now, but also look forward to the day that you can give them away because you can no longer use it and someone else would really appreciate it?

_____

_____

CONGRATULATIONS ON YOUR SUCCESS

ACCOMPLISHED
Generosity Dare 3

I accomplish this dare by _____

_____

How did you feel when you were doing this dare? _____

_____

Were you more focused on your loss or the joy of giving? (the loss / the joy)

I found it (easier / harder) than I thought it would be to give up something I want.

I found that there were (plenty of / some / not many) opportunities to do this dare.

Did you ever notice the opportunities after it was too late? Yes / No

Did you skip any opportunities to give up something you wanted? Yes / No

If Yes, why did you decide not to be generous in this case? _____

_____

Are you in the habit of sharing things you want for yourself? Yes / No

Circle the things that would be very hard for you to give up and fill in 2 of your own?

(money / time / belongings / weekend / pride / favorite food / cell phone /

_____ / _____)

Do you ever feel guilty or greedy when you decide not to share or be generous with the things that you want for yourself? Yes / No

CONGRATULATIONS ON YOUR SUCCESS

Generosity Dare 4

I accomplished this dare by _____

_____

What reward or payment did you refuse? _____

Did the person try to get you to take the reward or offer another? Yes / No

How did doing this dare make you feel? _____

How did the other person respond? _____

Opportunities to accomplish this dare were (very hard to find / easy to find / often realized after the opportunity was gone).

When opportunities to be helpful arose, the possibility of a reward or payment (was the first thing that crossed my mind / was usually somewhere in my thoughts / never even crossed my mind).

Did you find that you were more motivated to act on opportunities to help if the possibility of getting a reward or payment was higher? Yes / No

If you knew the possibility of a reward or payment was very unlikely, were you less motivated to act on the opportunity to help? Yes / No

Name the person that you think is the best at being generous with their time

by helping others and refuses any kind of reward. _____

The most important thing I learned from doing this dare was _____

_____

One benefit of doing this dare is _____

_____

CONGRATULATIONS ON YOUR SUCCESS

Generosity Dare 5

Giving compliments and refraining from insulting others for an entire day was (very difficult / somewhat difficult / not too hard / easy)

Giving compliments all day and refraining from insulting others made me feel _____

_____

Most of my compliments were (easy / hard) to come up with.

I found it easier to compliment on people's (physical / non-physical) qualities.

After an insult or negative comment was spoken about someone, did you accomplish following it up with 2 positive compliments about them?

Yes / No If Yes, what responses did you get from others? _____

_____

If No, what prevented you from accomplishing this? _____

_____

Did you manage to get the number of compliments to outweigh the insults by the end of the day? Yes / No

What did this dare teach you about yourself or others? _____

_____

_____

How would continuing to practice this dare benefit you? _____

_____

CONGRATULATIONS ON YOUR SUCCESS

Generosity Dare 6

Finding people being generous is (very difficult / hard / not too hard / easy).

Appreciating and acknowledging the generosity of others made me feel? _____

_____

What act of generosity most inspired you? _____

_____

What did you find people most willing to be generous with? (money / time / kind words /

personal belongings / other _____)

How did the people typically respond when you acknowledged them as a generous person

_____

Do you believe that being acknowledged for generous behaviors encourages and inspires the
person to continue being generous? Yes / No

For most people, I believe that being acknowledged or thanked for acts of generosity is
(extremely / very / somewhat / not too) important.

Did observing others being generous inspire you in any way? (Yes / No)

If Yes, how? _____

_____

List one generous act that you want to continue looking for, and hopefully find, others doing

so you can acknowledge their generosity? _____

_____

CONGRATULATIONS ON YOUR SUCCESS

CHAPTER REVIEW

What is your favorite quote from this chapter? Why?

_____

_____

Which of the dares was the hardest? Why?

_____ because _____

_____

_____

Which of the dares was the easiest? Why?

_____ because _____

_____

_____

Which dare made you feel the best about what you had done? Why?

_____ because _____

_____

_____

Which dare do you think you will try to do most often? Why?

_____ because _____

_____

_____

Which dare did you do the most? # _____

Which dare did you do the least? # _____

Which dare was easiest to remember? # _____ hardest? # _____

Which dare had the most shocking/dramatic results? # _____ why? _____

_____

Which dare or dares did people seem to notice when you did it? _____

What did you learn about yourself and/or others through this chapter's exercises?

_____

_____

_____

_____

_____

_____

_____

Can you think of another way to dare yourself in order to test or build-up this virtue?

_____

_____

_____

_____

_____

_____

_____

_____

_____

What was fun about these exercises? _____

_____

_____

What was not so fun? _____

_____

Use these 2 pages to keep notes during the week, jot down ideas or thoughts, or to evaluate your success. Set goals to help you accomplish the dares and goals for practicing them in the future.

_____

_____

_____

_____

_____

_____

_____

_____

_____

_____

_____

_____

_____

_____

_____

_____

_____

_____

_____

_____

_____

_____

_____

_____

_____

_____

_____

_____

_____

_____

_____

_____

_____

_____

_____

_____

_____

_____

_____

_____

_____

_____

_____

_____

_____

_____

_____

_____

_____

_____

_____

"It is not because things are difficult that we do not dare; it is because we do not dare that things are difficult."

~Seneca

"The wise man does not lay up his own treasures.
The more he gives to others, the more he has for his own."

Lao Tzu

CHAPTER 4

ACCEPTANCE

Acceptance: Acceptance is a complicated concept that often implies an agreement with and/or approval of something or someone. However, accepting a 10 o'clock bedtime doesn't mean we actually agree with it and accepting that a friend smokes cigarettes doesn't mean that we approve. Acceptance is better defined as our awareness and acknowledgment of what is **true**, regardless of our judgments or feelings about it.

Resistance: refuse to comply with; offer opposition. Denying or rejecting what is.

The Choice

Virtue: Acceptance

or

Vice: Resistance

The greatest two benefits of being accepting of others, yourself, and 'what is' are:

1.) _____

2.) _____

The two most detrimental consequences of resisting others, yourself, and 'what is' are:

1.) _____

2.) _____

Acceptance Agreement

I, _____, understand that being accepting is more beneficial to me than being resistant. Therefore, I agree to read the following chapter, answer the questions presented, complete any exercises, and attempt to accomplish as many dares as possible - as often as I can.

Signed: _____   Date: _____

Dare 1

"Think for yourselves and let others enjoy the privilege to do so too."

~ Voltaire

Dare to let others have their own opinions.

Has anyone ever tried to force a belief on you that you just didn't agree with? Often when people have a difference of opinions, each person sees their opinion as a fact and the other person's opinion as wrong or false. In an attempt to prove that we are right and convince someone to accept what we believe to be true, we begin presenting evidence to support what we think we know. However, having evidence that supports what we believe to be true does not necessarily make it true. It is important to remember that <u>what</u> we experience and <u>how we perceive</u> what we experience will determine our beliefs and opinions. Truth is, most of what we believe to be facts are really only beliefs or opinions with lots of supporting evidence. Consequently, what is absolutely true for you can be completely untrue for someone else. For example: A 5'2 woman and a 6'3 man both witness a 5'11 person steal a car. To the woman, the person was tall. To the man, the person was short. Their descriptions were both true and factual, but opposite due to a different starting perspective. When two people experience the same exact thing from the exact same perspective, they can still have a very different experience due to their past beliefs or opinions. Even knowing and accepting all this to be true, it will not always be easy to allow others to have their own opinions when it contradicts ours. When someone's opinion has a negative effect or impact on us, we may feel a strong need or urge to change their mind about what they think is true. Yet, if we want to enjoy the right to our own opinions or beliefs and want to be allowed to think for ourselves, we should be willing to allow everyone else to do the same.

To accomplish this dare: Allow others the freedom to think for themselves and resist trying to persuade anyone to accept your belief as true for them. Acknowledge that most of your thoughts are subjective opinions based off experience and are not necessarily facts or true for everyone. Practice stating your opinions as 'my opinion' and your beliefs as 'my belief.' Also try to refrain from supplying evidence to support your opinion or belief unless it is asked for. When a difference in opinions occurs, inquire into why they believe what they do and confirm that they have as much right to their opinion as you do to yours. Consider how or if you can both be right and perhaps agree to disagree.

Be Aware: When we don't argue for or try to provide support for our beliefs, people may perceive our acceptance of their opinion as evidence that they are right. Be careful not to fall into that trap. Accepting their opinion as 'their opinion' simply means...

1.) you acknowledge that there exists a difference in opinions
2.) you respect their right to have their own opinion
3.) you have no need to convince or persuade them otherwise

TRUTH AND DARE

When someone is pushing their belief or opinion on me in an attempt to change my mind,

I feel _____

Complete each of the following statements with N-for never, R-for rarely, S-for sometimes, O-for often, or A-for always.

I _____ enjoy the right to my own opinion and to choose who and what I like.

I _____ argue with people who do not agree with my opinions or beliefs.

I _____ 'agree to disagree.'

I am _____ willing to seeing things from someone else's perspective.

I _____ forget that my opinions are not always true for everyone else.

I _____ try persuading others to accept my opinion as true for them.

I _____ accept it when someone has a negative opinion or belief about me.

I _____ use evidence to prove my beliefs or opinions are right or true.

Mark each of the following as T-true or F-false

_____ In a disagreement between 2 people, 1 person is right and the other is wrong.

_____ It is important to me that people eventually see things from my perspective.

_____ Even when I allow someone's opinion to differ from mine, I still know that I am right and they are wrong.

_____ Helping someone to see the truth is more important than allowing them the freedom to believe something that I know is false.

_____ When I disagree with someone, it is beneficial to inquire into why they think or believe as they do.

Food for Thought: Did you think there was a right or wrong answer for the statements above? Your answers are not right or wrong, they are simply an expression of what is currently true for you. The statements were designed to reveal how accepting you are of other's opinions when they differ from your own and how willing you are to allow others the right to believe or think what they want. Hopefully, your answers will show you where you might want to focus your attention when trying to accomplish this dare.

Dare 2

"It is the mark of an educated mind to be able to entertain a thought without accepting it."

~Aristotle

Dare to challenge negative thoughts about yourself before accepting them as true.

Have you ever wondered why it is so easy to accept the negative things people say about you as true and how hard it is to take a compliment? How many negative thoughts about yourself do you think you have? Do you know from who or where those thoughts came from? Too often, the negative thoughts that we have about ourselves come from the people we love and admire the most. Perhaps a parent says to you, "You need to spend more time studying and less time playing video games because your grades are not as good as they should be." What you may take away from that comment may be, "I have to struggle to get good grades because I am not smart enough, and my mom doesn't accept me because I am stupid." Thoughts like "I am stupid," and "I am not good enough," can have a very negative effect on your school work as well as your personal relationships for a very long time. However, if you challenge negative thoughts about yourself before accepting them as true, they will most likely have little or no negative effect on you at all. What if you took away from your parents comment, "I am smart and I can do better if I just apply myself a little more," and "My mom loves me and just wants me to do the best I can"? Imagine how much more confident and motivated you would be if those were your thoughts instead. Truth is, many of the negative thoughts or beliefs we have about ourselves are not true at all. As for the few that are true, it is best to be accepting of them and continue to do what you can to improve on them.

To accomplish this dare: Use the following page to challenge 3 negative thoughts or beliefs you have about yourself and record the 1 that seems to be the most harmful or negative on the following page. You may also choose to challenge any beliefs that you have which keep you from being successful or happy. The process of challenging a belief or thought begins with an inquiry into how true the belief or negative thought really is. It then aims to prove that the opposite belief is actually (more) true in reality.

Be Aware: You may resist this process at first because many of the negative beliefs you have about yourself have been established as true for quite some time. Unfortunately, for every day that passes in which the belief goes unchallenged, the belief itself strengthens regardless of whether it is true or not. Holding on to negative beliefs about yourself, whether true or not true, will block you from the success, happiness, and love that you desire and deserve!

★★For more help challenging negative beliefs about yourself or thoughts that may be keeping you from the happiness or success you desire, look into *The Work* by Byron Katie.

What is the most harmful negative thought/belief about yourself that you want to challenge? Example: I am not worthy of success/Love or I am not smart/pretty enough.

I am _____

On a scale of 1-10, how true is this belief?

| 0 | 1 | 2 | 3 | 4 | 5 | 6 | 7 | 8 | 9 | 10 |

Not True   Rarely True   Sometimes True   Often True   Always True

Record how it makes you feel to have this belief or negative thought. _____

_____

What is the opposite of this belief? Example: I am not good enough → I am good enough

_____

Give 3 examples of times when this new/opposite belief or thought was true.

    1.) _____

    2.) _____

    3.) _____

List 2 reasons why it would be beneficial for you to accept this new/positive belief about yourself and let go of the old negative belief.

    1.) _____

    2.) _____

How willing are you to let go of the negative belief and replace it with one that can benefit your life and boost your Self-esteem? Not Willing / Somewhat Willing / Very Willing

List any other thoughts/beliefs about yourself that you may want to challenge. _____

_____

_____

Food for Thought: If you were unable to find support for the opposite belief or still find your first belief to be absolutely true, don't be discouraged. Sometimes our negative beliefs about ourselves have just enough truth in them to keep us from being able to let them go. In these cases, accepting the belief, instead of resisting it, is helpful. Yet, it is very important to limit the amount of energy you give to the negative thoughts/beliefs you have about yourself, and continue to seek, support, and value the positive thoughts more.

ACCEPTANCE
Dare 3

"**The weak can never forgive; forgiveness is an attribute of the strong.**"
~Mohandas Gandhi

Dare to forgive someone who you have not yet forgiven.

Telling someone that you forgive them is a fairly easy thing to do; meaning it is far more difficult. There are two main steps in the process of forgiveness: **Releasing and Ceasing**. The first step in the process is to <u>release</u> any anger, bitterness, or resentment we may have for someone who has hurt or wronged us. Easier said than done, right? Wrong! Buddha explained exactly how easy it is to accomplish this first step when he said, "Holding on to anger is like grasping a hot coal with the intent of throwing it at someone else; you are the one getting burned." In this quote, Buddha exposes that holding on to anger is a choice; a choice that causes us additional and unnecessary pain. At any point in time, we can choose to put the hot coal down or just drop it. Letting go of our negative feelings becomes easier once we acknowledge that we are responsible for them and realize how damaging they are to us. Unfortunately, letting go of the hot coal does not mean the pain or hurt will immediately disappear. However, we must release the hot coal before we can even begin the healing process. The second step of the forgiveness process is to <u>cease</u>, or stop, remembering the offense. To forgive requires us to give up seeking punishment, justice or revenge on someone who has hurt, offended, or wronged us. Ceasing means to put an end to something or leave it behind. So, if we have extended forgiveness to someone, we ought to refrain from rehashing or reliving it by leaving it in the past where it belongs. The great philosopher Confucius revealed the benefit of this step in his quote, "To be wronged is nothing, unless you continue to remember it." Truth is, refusing to forgive others is a choice to punish ourselves. When we come to understand that forgiving others of their offense actually releases us from its bond, forgiveness becomes not only the logical thing to do – but also the easiest.

To accomplish this dare: Extend forgiveness to someone who has hurt, offended or wronged you. Use the questions on the following page to help you release any negative feelings you have for someone. Then, cease remembering it by committing to put it behind you and refrain from ever bringing it back up. Try to find the courage to let the person know that you are giving them your forgiveness. Assure them that you are releasing all negative feelings and ceasing to remember the offense from now on. If you can't think of anyone to forgive, you can use an event from the past in which you did forgive someone in order to accomplish the dare.

Be Aware: The main goals of forgiveness are to heal the wounds and restore our peace. Sure, it would be nice if forgiving others also restored our relationships, but we can't expect that it always will. All we can really do is give our forgiveness to others; if they accept it or want it is completely up to them.

TRUTH AND DARE

Name someone who has angered, offended, wronged or hurt you. _____

Describe exactly what they did. _____

_____

Circle any negative feelings that you have felt as a result of what they did.

Angry	Embarrassed	Offended	Hurt
Wronged	Disappointed	Cheated	Deceived
Depressed	Frustrated	Resentful	Abused
Ignored	Manipulated	Insulted	Rejected

Write 2 sentences that describe how you feel or how you felt when it happened. Use the negative feelings circled above or any other negative feeling you may have experienced.

1.) _____

2.) _____

Take responsibility for all of your negative feelings by using each one, circled above, to complete the following sentence:

"I am **choosing** to hold on to my feeling of being _____."

Acknowledge the benefit of releasing all of your negative feelings by using each one to complete the following sentence.

"If I release my feeling of being _____, I would probably feel _____

_____

What will most likely be the result if you choose to continue remembering this offense?

_____

What would the result most likely be if you choose to cease remembering the offense?

_____

Make Your Choice: I choose to (hold on to / release) my negative feelings and I am committed to (continuing / ceasing) to remember the offense.

ACCEPTANCE
Dare 4

"Never ruin an apology with an excuse."   ~Kimberly Johnson

"Justifying a fault doubles it."   ~French Proverb

Dare to accept responsibility for your actions.

Do you know what the difference is between these two sentences: 1.) The dog ate my homework. 2.) I let the dog eat my homework. The answer is accountability. In the first sentence, it's the dog's fault I don't have my homework and in the second sentence it's ultimately my fault. When we fail to do what we are supposed to do or do something we wish we hadn't done or shouldn't have done, we often make excuses for our actions or redirect the blame onto someone or something else. Even though most of the excuses we use to justify our actions are quite creative, they are rarely ever the truth and often lack a humble apology. For example, when we forget to do a chore and a parent calls us down about it, we often offer a lie instead of an apology. "I was just about to do it," or "I was waiting until the garbage bag was completely full so not to waste bags." Accepting responsibility for our actions would cause us to respond with a simple "I am sorry, I will do it right now," or "I am sorry, I forgot." If you're late for work or school because you over slept or took too long getting ready, what makes you think that blaming it on a train or traffic is somehow more acceptable? Truth is, there is nothing more respectable and acceptable than a humble apology and the truth. "I am sorry, I didn't intend to be late," or "I am sorry, I had trouble getting out of the house on time" is far more believable and excusable. Trying to justify ourselves to others, making excuses, and redirecting blame are all defense mechanisms that we use to make ourselves feel better or to prevent ourselves from feeling guilty for what we did or didn't do. Unfortunately, they rarely ever work and often add even more conflict or tension to the situation and/or relationship. The key to avoiding feeling guilty or ashamed of your actions can be found in Elbert Hubbard's quote, "Don't make excuses – make good." The surest and quickest way to make good is to apologize, provide a reason (not an excuse) only if required, and then do whatever you can to make things better.

To accomplish this dare: On 3 different occasions, accept responsibility for your actions instead of trying to justify them, making up an excuse, or redirecting blame. It is as simple as – "If you mess up – fess up!" Whenever you find yourself trying to explain or justify what you have done or didn't do, stop and accept responsibility for your actions. If you find yourself searching for a good excuse – stop and use the truth instead. When you catch yourself redirecting blame, ask yourself "What part did I play in this situation and what should or could I have done differently?" Try to avoid judging your actions as right or wrong. Instead, acknowledge how much better you will feel if you offer a sincere apology and focus on 'making things good.'

I (always / often / sometimes / rarely / never) try to justify or defend my actions when I make a mistake or fail to do what I am supposed to do.

I (always / often / sometimes / rarely / never) make up excuses for my actions instead of telling the truth.

List 2 reasons why you would use a made up excuse instead of the truth.

1.) _____

2.) _____

I (always / often / sometimes / rarely / never) try to redirect blame on to someone else instead of taking responsibility for my actions.

Saying 'I am sorry' is (always / often / sometimes / rarely / never) hard for me to say.

List 2 benefits that may come from offering a humble apology and the truth when your actions are hurtful or disrespectful to someone.

1.) _____

2.) _____

When you are hurt or disappointed by someone's actions, how do you feel if they defend their actions, make excuses for what they have done, or redirect the blame back on you?

_____

How do typically respond to them? _____

When you are hurt or disappointed by someone's actions, how do you feel when they give you a sincere apology and an honest reason why they did what they did? _____

_____

How do you think you would respond to them? _____

_____

What was the most outrageous excuse you have ever made up to avoid getting in trouble and

what were the results? _____

_____

Dare 5

"**We can not change anything until we accept it.**"   ~Carl Gustav Jung

"**Only by acceptance of something, can you alter it.**"   ~T.S. Elliot

Dare to be accepting of what IS instead of resisting it.

When things aren't the way we think they should be or differ from how we want them to be, we often spend a lot of time and energy resisting what can't be changed. Dwelling on, complaining about, fighting against, and denying something that has already happened are just a few examples of how we resist what we don't want to be true. Wishing things were different is also a popular form of resistance. However, we will never change what IS by wishing it never was. Truth is, what we resist – persists! **Resistance** is an <u>emotional reaction</u> which keeps us attached to the past and destined to continually relive it. The more we resist what we want to change, the more likely it is to stay the same. **Acceptance** is <u>a rational response</u> which acknowledges what IS. In other words, acceptance is the acknowledgment that – "It IS what it IS!" William James once said, "Acceptance of what has happened is the first step to overcoming the consequences of any misfortune." He understood that acceptance of what IS forces us to focus less on what has happened and more on what we can do about it. Once we stop resisting what was, acceptance allows us to start considering what can be.

To accomplish this dare: Practice replacing resistance with acceptance. To do this, use this simple exercise at the first sign of resistance: **So What – Now What?** This exercise will help you to accept and emotionally detach from what was so you can explore what can be. When you say – So What, your goal is to acknowledge and accept what IS true and agree to temporarily let your feelings about it go so you can clearly think about what you can do about it. When you ask – Now What, your goal is to explore all your options and consider how you would like to respond to what IS. Complete the So What – Now What exercise on the following page. Then, use the So What – Now What exercise on 2 more occasions within a 3 day period.

Be Aware: The reason people struggle with accepting what they don't want to be true is because they believe accepting something means you have given up trying to change it. For example, if I accept that I am 10 pounds overweight than that's it – I can't change it. But, if I refuse to accept it, fight against it, cover it up, complain about it, or deny it… the 10 pounds may magically go away. It is very important to remember that acceptance is not submission – it is acknowledging what IS true. The faster you accept what IS, the quicker you can change it. Fighting against what you don't want, keeps you from getting what you do! Acceptance begins when resistance ends.

So What – Now What Exercise

Scenario 1: Predict the most likely outcome.
A waitress gives great service to her guest but gets a very bad tip.
<u>Resistance Reaction</u>: She dwells on it, stays mad, complains about it to everyone and gives bad service for the rest of the night.
Outcome = _____.
<u>Acceptance Response</u>: "So What? I got a bad tip. Now What? The rest of my tables may appreciate great service and tip me well."
Outcome = _____.

Scenario 2: Create a resistance reaction and outcome.

You help a friend to get a job at the place where you have been working for over a year already. They have the same job title and experience as you but will be making $1.00 per hour more than you do.
Resistance Reaction: _____.

Outcome = _____.

<u>Acceptance Response</u>: "So What? They make more than I do. Now What? I can continue to do my best at work and ask for a raise or I can look for a job that will pay me what I want to make." Outcome = I get the raise or I find a better job.

Scenario 3: Create an acceptance response and outcome.
You have plans to meet some friends at the beach but your mom's car broke down and she has to borrow yours so she can get to work.
<u>Resistance reaction:</u> You argue with your mom, complain how unfair it is, blame her for ruining your plans, and throw your keys in anger. Outcome = you get punished, she takes your car, and she cries the whole way to work.
<u>Acceptance Response</u>: "So What? _____,

Now What? _____ "

Outcome = _____.

Identify each of the following as either resistance (R) or acceptance (A) phrases. The resistant phrases will provide you with examples of opportunities to accomplish the dare.

_____ I still can't believe that...   _____ The best thing for me to do now is...

_____ I am not happy about this, but...   _____ This can not really be happening...

_____ I wish I would have...   _____ It is not fair that she/he gets to...

_____ I hate that I have to...   _____ I can't change what Is, but I can...

_____ I think my best response would be... _____ It would have been better if...

_____ I won't or can't let this go because... _____ It is what it IS, so I guess I should...

_____ I will never forgive you for...   _____ The past is for learning; not re-living!

ACCEPTANCE
Dare 6

"If there is anything that we wish to change in others, we should first examine it and see whether it is not something that could better be changed in ourselves."

~Carl Gustav Jung

Dare to seek within yourself for what you dislike in others.

Have you ever heard the saying, "The negative things you say about another actually says more about you than it does about them"? The same can be said about the negative things you see in others. The great philosopher and psychologist Carl Jung also said, "Everything that irritates us about others can lead us to an understanding of ourselves." Just like a mirror reflects what is in front of it by using light, what is happening outside of us will reflect what is happening inside of us. Truth is, a strong negative emotion or response to other's behaviors are often like light rays that allow our own flaws to be reflected back to us for us to see. The bad news is, if we look within ourselves for the things we don't like in others, we might just learn something about ourselves that may be hard to accept. The good news is, what self reflection uncovers is a window of opportunity for you to make desired improvements. So, if someone does something that bothers you but it doesn't really affect you too much, then it is not likely something you struggle with internally. On the other hand, if you catch someone being hypocritical and it really gets you angry and you can't seem to get your mind off of it, you have most likely discovered something that you don't like about yourself or may need to work on. By using your external world as a mirror for Self-Reflection, you will be slower to find flaws in others and quicker at improving on them within yourself.

To accomplish this dare: Learn something about yourself by letting your emotions guide you to look within when something external is disturbing you. You may discover that someone's personality flaw or obnoxious behavior which irritates or angers you is something that you are struggling with yourself. It doesn't have to be specific; it may be a general frustration. For example, if someone's procrastinating drives you crazy, ask "Where am I procrastinating?" If you get really angry when people judge you, ask "Who do I judge?" If someone's betrayal has you wanting revenge, consider if you have ever betrayed them. On 2 occasions, look within by answering the 3 questions at the bottom of the next page and then complete the sentence about what you have learned about yourself.

Be Aware: This dare is designed to help you be more accepting of the flaws in others by revealing the same flaws in yourself. Try not to focus on the flaws as much as you focus on what you can do to improve on them. There may be times when your negative feelings or strong opinions about other's behaviors do not reflect a negative behavior or quality in yourself. In these cases, expect that the experience still presents an opportunity for you to learn and grow.

Name one person who can sometimes irritate you? _____

What is the most common thing they do that really gets on your nerves? _____
_____

Why do you think this bothers you so much and what emotions does it bring out in you?
_____

Could this be a reflection (something you have done yourself) that you might want to work on improving? Yes / No

What lesson could this experience/person be trying to teach you? _____
_____

Name one general thing that really irritates you and what feelings does it tend to create? (Ex. Littering, negative attitudes, criticism, back-stabbing, gossip, lying, bullying, ect.)

_____   _____

Could this be a reflection (something you have done yourself) that you might want to work on improving? Yes / No

What lesson could this experience/person be trying to teach you? _____
_____

What benefits do you believe can come from looking for your own flaws instead of focusing on others? _____
_____

Ask yourself these 3 questions on 2 separate occasions when you get angry, irritated, or frustrated. It could be at someone, a specific behavior, an attitude, or any general situation. Then, consider and record what you have learned about yourself from the experience.

   1.) What is it about this experience/person that I don't like or would want to change?

   2.) What could this experience/person be reflecting about me?

   3.) What could this experience/person be trying to teach me or what can I learn from it?

What I learned about myself from this experience/person is _____
_____

Acceptance Dare 1

How did you feel when you were doing this dare? _____

_____

Allowing others to have their own opinion without trying to defend my opinion or persuade them to change their mind was (easy / a little challenging / difficult).

During the day, did you ever state something as a fact but then realized that it may not be true for everyone or that it is actually just an opinion?   Yes / No

How effective were you at stating your opinions as 'my opinion' and what benefit can this

expression produce? _____

_____

_____

When someone's opinion opposes mine but has no real impact on me or my reputation, I am (more / less) likely to dispute it or try to persuade them.

When someone's opinion opposes mine and it directly affects me or my reputation, I am (more / less) likely to dispute it or try to persuade them.

What feelings or thoughts do you have about 'agreeing to disagree'?

_____

_____

List 2 benefits produced by allowing others the right to think for themselves.

1.) _____

2.) _____

CONGRATULATIONS ON YOUR SUCCESS

Acceptance Dare 2

How did challenging your negative beliefs about yourself make you feel?

_____

Of the 3 beliefs that you challenged, how many of them were actually **less** true than the

opposite belief? _____

Have you let go of any beliefs as a result of what you learned? Yes / No

Where or Who did most of your negative beliefs about yourself come from?

_____

_____

Why do you think this source has such an impact on you and what can you do about it?

_____

_____

What does having these negative beliefs about yourself keep you from achieving or experiencing?
(What do they cost you? peace? success? health?)

_____

_____

It was (easy / somewhat easy / somewhat difficult / difficult) to find evidence to support
the positive and opposite belief about myself.

How can challenging negative thoughts about yourself benefit you? _____

_____

Are you willing to replace your negative thoughts for positive ones? Yes / No

CONGRATULATIONS ON YOUR SUCCESS

4 ACCEPTANCE

ACCOMPLISHED
Acceptance Dare 3

Who did you chose to extend forgiveness to and for what? _____

_____

What negative feelings did you have to release in order to forgive them and how strong were

these feelings? _____

_____

Were you able to release these feelings? Yes / Somewhat / Not really

If Yes, how easy/difficult was it? If Somewhat, did it help? If No, why not? _____

_____

Did you let the person know you have decided to forgive them? Yes / No

If Yes, what was there response? _____

_____

Are you committed to cease/stop reliving or rehashing the offense? Yes / No

Which will likely be harder for you: Keeping the negative feelings released or refusing to
keep it in the past and not bring it back up? Explain why.

_____

_____

How can continuing to practice this dare benefit you throughout your life? _____

_____

CONGRATULATIONS ON YOUR SUCCESS

Acceptance Dare 4

Describe 2 of the 3 occasions when you refrained from justifying your actions, making up an excuse, or redirecting blame onto someone else.

Occasion 1: What action did you accept responsibility for; what did you do?

_____

What did you most want to do when your action had a negative effect?

    1.) Justify, defend or explain your action,

    2.) Make up an excuse or lie to avoid getting in trouble,

    3.) Re-direct blame onto someone or something else to avoid responsibility.

What did you do instead? _____

_____

Occasion 2: What action did you accept responsibility for; what did you do?

_____

What did you most want to do when your action had a negative effect?

    1.) Justify, defend or explain your action,

    2.) Make up an excuse or lie to avoid getting in trouble,

    3.) Re-direct blame onto someone or something else to avoid responsibility.

What did you do instead? _____

_____

How did doing this dare make you feel? _____

I believe that the greatest benefit of using a humble apology and the Truth instead of justifying

yourself, making up excuses, or re-directing blame is _____

_____

CONGRATULATIONS ON YOUR SUCCESS

ACCEPTANCE

4

Acceptance Dare 5

When doing the So What – Now What exercise, was the resistance reaction or the acceptance response harder to create? _____

Why? _____

I accomplished this dare when I noticed I was feeling some resistance about _____

_____.

My initial or normal resistance reaction to this event was or would have been _____

_____

and the outcome would have likely been _____.

Instead, I applied the exercise by saying, So What _____

_____, Now What _____

_____ and the outcome was _____

This dare helped me to see that I: (Use a check to indicate which are true)

_____ dwell on the things that bother me longer than I should.

_____ complain about things I can not change or do not like more than I need to.

_____ fight against what IS by arguing about what I don't think is fair or right.

_____ deny what IS by ignoring it or refusing to deal with it.

_____ spend too much time wishing things were different or thinking about how they should have been.

What did accomplishing this dare teach you and will you continue to do it? _____

_____

_____

CONGRATULATIONS ON YOUR SUCCESS

TRUTH AND DARE

Acceptance Dare 6

How hard was it to look within yourself for the things you didn't like in others? (extremely hard / somewhat difficult / not too hard / very easy)

(People / Behaviors / Attitudes / General situations) seem to get me irritated, angry, or frustrated most often.

When I allowed my negative emotions to lead me to reflect inward, I answered the 3 questions and completed the sentence as follows. (Choose your favorite of the 2 occasion you recorded to fill in this part.)

1.) What is it about this experience/person that I don't like or would want to change?
_____

2.) What could this experience/person be reflecting about me? _____
_____

3.) What could this experience/person be trying to teach me or what can I learn from it?
_____
_____

What I learned about myself from this experience/person is _____
_____
_____

What do you believe accomplishing this dare taught you and how will you continue to use it? _____
_____

The hardest part of this dare was _____
_____

CONGRATULATIONS ON YOUR SUCCESS

CHAPTER REVIEW

What is your favorite quote from this chapter? Why?

_____

_____

Which of the dares was the hardest? Why?

_____ because _____

_____

_____

Which of the dares was the easiest? Why?

_____ because _____

_____

_____

Which dare made you feel the best about what you had done? Why?

_____ because _____

_____

_____

Which dare do you think you will try to do most often? Why?

_____ because _____

_____

_____

Which dare did you do the most? # _____

Which dare did you do the least? # _____

Which dare was easiest to remember? # _____ hardest? # _____

Which dare had the most shocking/dramatic results? # _____ why? _____

_____

Which dare or dares did people seem to notice when you did it? _____

What did you learn about yourself and/or others through this chapter's exercises?

_____

_____

_____

_____

_____

_____

_____

Can you think of another way to dare yourself in order to test or build-up this virtue?

_____

_____

_____

_____

_____

_____

_____

_____

What was fun about these exercises? _____

_____

_____

What was not so fun? _____

_____

Use these 2 pages to keep notes during the week, jot down ideas or thoughts, or to evaluate your success. Set goals to help you accomplish the dares and goals for practicing them in the future.

"It is not because things are difficult that we do not dare; it is because we do not dare that things are difficult."

~Seneca

"Acceptance is not submission; it is acknowledgment of the facts of a situation. Then deciding what you are going to do about it."

Kathleen Casey Theisen

CHAPTER 5

ENCOURAGE/INSPIRE

Encourage: give courage, confidence, or hope to; stimulate with help or reward.

Discourage: deprive of courage, confidence, or energy; inhibit or seek to prevent.

As defined by The Oxford illustrated Dictionary

The Choice

Virtue: Encouraging/Inspiring

or

Vice: Discouraging/Critical

The greatest two benefits of being encouraging are:

1.) _____

2.) _____

The two most detrimental consequences of being discouraging or critical are:

1.) _____

2.) _____

Encourage/Inspire Agreement

I, _____, understand that being encouraging and inspiring are more beneficial to me than being discouraging and critical. Therefore, I agree to read the following chapter, answer the questions presented, complete any exercises, and attempt to accomplish as many dares as possible – as often as I can.

Signed: _____   Date: _____

Dare 1

"**Character is the sum and total of a person's choices.**"   ~ P.B. Fitzwater

Dare to acknowledge and encourage the good character of others.

Our character is not something we are born with; we build it and define it a little bit more every day. Some days we refine it by being more virtuous than usual and other days we stain it by acting carelessly. As the quote above implies, our intentions do not determine our character. Instead, it's our choices, visible in our behaviors, which define and expose our 'Character'. Johann Wolfgang von Goethe, who was a great German writer and philosopher, once said, "To think is easy. To act is difficult. To act as one thinks is the most difficult." Truth is, people do not judge you according to your intentions; they judge you according to your actions. You may be surprised by how often your intentions are different from your actions. If you have good intentions to do something but for whatever reason your actions do not follow accordingly, you are 'out of alignment'. It is just like a car that is not aligned very well, letting go of the wheel will cause you to get off track or head in the opposite direction. When our actions are out of alignment more often than they should be, our character quickly becomes the opposite of who we want it to be. The good news is, we have the power and the ability to create our character just as we would like it to be. By aligning our actions with our best intentions daily, our good character can be securely established. However, the bad news is best explained in a famous quote from Thomas Paine. He said, "Character is much easier kept than recovered." Trying to repair your character is very difficult because people remember the 'bad' things you do, say, or cause them to feel much longer than you want them to. Acting 'outside your character' because you are having a bad day may not seem like a big deal to you, but to someone else it may cause them to question which character best reflects the real you. Finding someone who is in 'alignment' consistently enough to have established themselves as a person of good character is often very difficult. However, taking the time to acknowledge people when their actions seem to reflect their good intentions may be just the encouragement they need to continue practicing the behaviors that can securely establish their good character.

To accomplish this dare: Choose to acknowledge and encourage 3 people who you believe have securely established their good character. These 3 people should be people who are consistently displaying virtuous behaviors and who rarely act 'outside of their character.' They seem to know exactly Who They Are and appear to have their intentions and actions regularly aligned. Either in a letter or through a friendly conversation, acknowledge what qualities you admire most about them and try to use examples of when you witnessed it as evidence. Encourage them to continue valuing their character by expressing how they inspire you and how they are a positive influence in the lives of others.

On a scale from 1 to 10, with 1 being 'not aligned' and 10 being 'very aligned,' how aligned do believe your intentions and actions are on a regular basis?

(Circle one)   1   2   3   4   5   6   7   8   9   10

Which of the 3 character quotes on the previous page is your favorite? Why?

_____

_____

List the names of the 3 people you will choose to accomplish this dare with?

1)_____   2)_____   3)_____

Finding 3 people of good character was (very easy / easy / somewhat hard / hard).

For each person, list the qualities you admire most about them or give the main reason why you chose them.

    1.) _____

    2.) _____

    3.) _____

Do you have specific examples of when you witnessed their good character? Yes / No

What are your feelings about acknowledging and encouraging their good character? _____

_____

If someone chose to accomplish this dare on you, what would they most likely say and how do you think it would you make you feel? _____

_____

Food for Thought: Did you know that the qualities you admire the most in others are qualities you also have? That is why you are able to recognize and admire that quality in them. Being unaware of that quality within yourself only means you have not yet acknowledged it is there or it's not as dominant as you would like it to be. When you choose to see it – you can then choose to build on it and expose it to others. This is also true for qualities you do not like in others. The things that people do that really irritate you are often things that you do as well. What others do that bothers us often reflects something we could improve about ourselves. The virtues and vices we see or recognize in others should motivate us to explore ourselves for those same traits.

Dare 2

"Kind words can be short and easy to speak, but their echoes are truly endless."
~Mother Teresa

Dare to acknowledge the kind words and actions of others.

From a very young age, we learn that every action has a reaction. We do something, and our parents respond. If the response is positive, we accept it as a reward or reinforcement that what we did was good. We are very likely to repeat these behaviors because the reactions or responses we get when we do it make us feel good. If the response is negative, we determine that our behavior was bad and expect that a punishment will likely follow. We will attempt to avoid repeating these behaviors because the negative responses cause pain, loss, or unhappy feelings. Both positive and negative feedback from others, especially about the things we do, is very important to the majority of people. Truth is, many of our habits, behaviors, and even our values are the result of all the rewards, punishments, and responses we have received in the past from the people we love. Therefore, when we acknowledge the kind words and actions of others, we are actually encouraging them to continue or repeat that behavior. This dare aims to not only cause you to look for and acknowledge the kind words and actions of others in order to encourage or inspire them, but will also help you to appreciate the little things people do which often go unnoticed and unappreciated.

To accomplish this dare: Within a 1 day period, find and acknowledge 3 different people for their kind words or actions. If you see someone holding the door open for others, acknowledge their patience and kindness. If you hear someone complimenting or encouraging someone else, acknowledge their optimism and supportiveness. If you see someone being helpful or sharing, acknowledge their generosity. If someone is using polite language or patiently waiting for their turn to speak, acknowledge their respectfulness. If someone is standing up for a friend, acknowledge their loyalty. To be really effective at encouraging a specific behavior, try to state the virtue they are displaying and not the action itself. "Good job, Mike" will not be as encouraging as "Mike, standing up for your friend shows me that you are a loyal person and that is a really great quality to have."

Be Aware: It is just as easy to reinforce behaviors that shouldn't be repeated as it is to reinforce behaviors that should. Laughing at someone who is cutting up in class by acting like a clown or by disrespecting the teacher may not seem like a big deal. However, laughing at them may be their desired response and can actually encourage that person to repeat the behavior. In the end, the result or consequence of their behavior may turn out to be not very funny at all.

When I catch people doing or saying kind things, I most often

    a.) think to myself how nice they are but don't tell them anything

    b.) acknowledge them, but in a joking way

    c.) judge their behavior as fake or believe they are just trying to suck up to someone

    d.) mock them or make them feel silly or guilty for doing or saying something nice

    e.) acknowledge their behavior and encourage them to continue it

    f.) Other _____

How do you feel when you are complimenting, encouraging, or trying to inspire someone? Circle any that are true and add one of your own.

(awkward / uncomfortable / fake / silly / comfortable / good inside / proud / _____)

How do you feel when others acknowledge and encourage your kind words and actions? Circle any that are true and add one of your own.

(awkward / uncomfortable / fake / silly / comfortable / good inside / proud / _____)

What was the nicest thing anyone has ever said to you or done for you and who was it?

_____

_____

_____

Name 3 people who have impressed you by doing something extremely kind, generous or helpful or perhaps inspired you with their kind words. Next to their name, write what qualities or virtues you believe caused them to do what they did or what was most likely their reason for doing it.

    1.) _____

    2.) _____

    3.) _____

Food for Thought: Getting positive feedback or a positive response is great and may be effective at encouraging someone to repeat the behavior enough to call it a habit. However, becoming dependant on positive feedback to determine your actions may cause you to lose the motivation to continue the desirable behavior when it is not reinforced. If you avoid the behaviors that best represent the person you want to be because they are not being acknowledged or reinforced, you have placed more value in the reward than in the person doing the action – You. As a child, rewards and positive reinforcement are key factors for learning and developing good behaviors; but as an adult, they shouldn't be required – only appreciated.

Dare 3

"You will make more friends in one week by getting yourself interested in other people than you can in a year by trying to get other people interested in you."

~ Arnold Bennett

Dare to encourage someone to tell you more about themselves.

When we first meet someone, we typically use questions to learn what we want to know about them. We may ask, "Where are you from, how old are you, or what kind of activities are you interested in?" At this point, you show a real interest in the other person because you are trying to determine whether you want to enter into a relationship with them or not. Rather quickly, we stop asking them questions about themselves and start assuming we know who they are based on what they say or do. Unfortunately, the more we assume to know about someone, the less likely we will be to inquire about or discover - 'who they really are'. As a result, what we know about others is often limited to a few basic facts, some shared personal experiences, and a whole bunch of assumptions that may not even be true. Why do we know so little about so many of the people in our lives? Sometimes, we are just not interested enough to ask. Other times, it may be because we assume to know who others are, and we never bother to question what we believe to be true about them. Occasionally, what little we know about someone is the result of their unwillingness to let us know who they really are. Most of the time, however, the reason we know so little about others is because we are more interested in telling others who we are than we are in learning who they are. While trying to convince others that we are interesting and worth knowing, we fail to remember that they are too! Truth is, to really know someone means to know their dreams, fears, beliefs, passions, feelings, struggles, and desires. If we want to know who our parents, friends, and partners really are, the best thing we can do is ask them! By being sincerely interested in what is important to them, how they think, or why they feel the way they do, we not only learn more about them but we also confirm how important they are to us.

To accomplish this dare: Get to know at least 3 people a little bit better than you already do. Complete the exercise on the following page on a good friend to see how well you know them. Then, use the questions from the exercise as a reference or guide to help you get to know 2 people on a deeper and more personal level. When choosing the 2 people you want to accomplish this dare on, try to pick one person you think you know fairly well and one person you don't know as well as you would like.

Be Aware: If you have already made assumptions about someone and then begin to inquire into who they really are, you may struggle with believing any information that conflicts with what you think you already know. If this happens, assume the more favorable information to be true!

TRUTH AND DARE

Most of what I know about the people in my life seems to be based on:

    a.) General facts
    b.) Personal experiences
    c.) Assumptions resulting from what they say and do
    d.) What other people tell me about themselves
    e.) Rumors

I believe that I take (a lot of / a good amount of / some / very little) interest in getting to know who others really are.

I believe that the reason people don't really know much about others is because _____

_____

Exercise: Find a friend who is willing to answer a few very personal questions. Before you meet with them, finish the following sentences with what you think your friend would say. Then, read the sentences to them one at a time and ask them to complete the sentences as honestly as possible. Record their responses on the second line.

Who did you find to help you complete this exercise? _____

Finish the following sentences with what you think this person would say.

    1.) The thing that I am most afraid of is _____

            _____

    2.) The thing I look most forward to achieving is _____

            _____

    3.) If I could do anything I wanted for a career it would be _____

            _____

    4.) The thing I struggle with the most is _____

            _____

    5.) What I want most in my life right now is _____

            _____

    6.) What I am most thankful/grateful for would be _____

            _____

    7.) If I could improve one thing about myself, it would be _____

            _____

Dare 4

"Never look down on someone unless you are helping them up."   ~Jesse Jackson

Dare to be empathetic instead of sympathetic.

People often confuse the words sympathy and empathy. Simply put, sympathy is a feeling or expression of sorrow or pity for someone who is suffering from pain or distress; whereas empathy is an understanding and identification with another's pain or distress. In other words, sympathy is a feeling of "I don't want to be in your shoes," and empathy is the act of putting yourself in another's shoes so that you can understand better what they are going through and/or how they are feeling. Sympathy is a negative judgment, which comes from the mind, which creates a feeling of pity; empathy is identification, which stems from the heart, which creates a feeling of compassion. Imagine that there is someone at your school who has just moved to your area, has no friends, and appears to be very shy. Sympathy might cause you to feel bad or sorry for them; yet, at the same time you may be feeling happy that you're not in their shoes. However, empathy would cause you to consider what it would be like to actually be this person and will often make you think thoughts like, "What would I want someone to do or say to me if I was the new kid in school." A sympathetic person often feels unable to help and takes on the negative feelings that the other person is having. Friedrich Nietzsche acknowledged this in his quote, "Pity makes suffering contagious." An empathic person, on the other hand, is motivated to be supportive and encouraging from a positive, emotional perspective. Truth is, an empathic person can be far more beneficial to a person going through a difficult time than a sympathetic person may be. Think about it! Would you prefer someone who feels sorry for you, looks down on you with pity, or sees you as broken and/or weak; or would you prefer someone who tries to understand what you are going through, believes in your ability to get through the situation, lends a helpful hand – if possible, and encourages you the best they can? We often, unknowingly and unintentionally, reinforce a person's weakness when we pity them. When we are empathetic to people going through a tough time or suffering from lack or a loss, extending our compassion, encouragement, and support can help them feel empowered and not so alone.

To accomplish this dare: Use the exercise on the following page to practice replacing sympathy with empathy. Then, try to think about someone you feel sorrow for or pity, replace the sympathy you feel with empathy, and record it on the accomplished dare page. If you can't think of someone or an event doesn't occur in the next 7 days, then you are able to use a past experience to accomplish this dare.

<u>Use the acronym of the word ABLE below to practice replacing sympathy with empathy.</u>

A – *Acknowledge* what the person is going through and what feelings they may be having by imagining what it would be like to be in their shoes. (Remember: trying to imagine what they are going through and what they are feeling does not mean you need to take on their feelings or try to solve their problems.)

B – *Believe* the person has the ability to deal with or get through their situation and that what they are going through provides them with an opportunity to grow and learn.

L – *Lend* a hand if you can. Offer your assistance and let them know they can count on you to be there for them if there is anything they need.

E - *Encourage* them. Let them know that you believe in their ability to get through their difficult time even though it looks and feels impossible at the moment.

Example: Your best friend just found out that his/her parents are getting a divorce and your friend is taking it really hard. Sympathy: "That's horrible. I am so sorry you are hurting."

Empathy: (A) – I can imagine how shocked, scared, confused, and saddened my friend probably is by this news. (B) – I know (s)he will get through this and that it's probably going to work out well in the end. (L) – "Let me know if there is anything I can do to help you. I am here for you if you just want to talk or if you need anything- please just ask." (E) – "I know you are feeling confused, hurt, and scared. That's normal considering what you are going through. I also know that you can and will get through this."

<u>For each of the following scenarios, consider what the sympathetic response would be and then go through the ABLE steps above to create an empathetic response. Then, record 1 of your responses in the space provided below.</u>

Scenario 1: The best running back on the football team broke his ankle in the first game of his senior year. Now, he is out for the year and this injury could cost him his scholarship.
Scenario 2: A good friend of yours just got caught cheating on their math exam. Not only did their grade fall from a B to an F, but they may even get suspended from school.
Scenario 3: Your best friend's boyfriend/girlfriend of 3 years just broke up with them 3 days before the prom and has already found another date. Your best friend is devastated!

Sympathetic response: _____

Empathetic response:

(A): _____

(B): _____

(L): _____

(E): _____

Food for Thought: There are some people who seem to always want us to feel sorry for them. These people often have the 'poor me' attitude and a 'victim mentality' because they think it serves them. However, it doesn't. Being empathetic towards them may be difficult because they tend to want to hold on to their pain and suffering. Yet, it is always more beneficial to them, as well as yourself, to be empathetic instead of having pity for them.

Dare 5

"Flatter me, and I may not believe you. Criticize me, and I may not forgive you. Ignore me, and I may not like you. Encourage me, and I will not forget you! "
~William Arthur Ward

Dare to encourage someone to take at least one action toward accomplishing a goal or a dream.

Have you ever really wanted to do or accomplish something but never succeeded because you kept putting it off? Unfortunately, many people fail to accomplish their goals or dreams because they let laziness, fear, or excuses keep them from ever getting started. Truth is, what is never started, can never be finished. For some people, procrastination is evidence that the accomplishment is not really all that important to them or perhaps it isn't worth the effort required. For others, procrastination is evidence that there exists an underlying fear or belief that is blocking the motivation and willingness they need to even begin. These people can have the desire and the ability required to achieve their goal or dream, but they inevitably fail because they never actually begin. Fear of failure, fear of success, fear of looking stupid, fear of rejection, fear of not being good enough or smart enough, and fear of letting others down are just a few of the fears that can hold someone back from the success they desire. They will use excuses like, "It would take too long," "It's too risky," "I can't afford to do it," "I don't deserve it," "It's too big," "It's just a dream," or "I am too busy" to justify why they don't even try. Encouraging these people to "Just Do It," or "Go for it," will not guarantee their success, but it may be just what they need to get started.

To accomplish this dare: Encourage someone to take one action towards accomplishing their desired goal or dream. Ask at least 5 people, "What is something you would like to do or accomplish but you really haven't put much effort into it yet?" or "What goal would you love to reach but have given up on or doubt you will ever achieve." Then, choose the person who you think will benefit the most from your encouragement. Try not to pick someone who is just being lazy or whose goal doesn't seem to be all that important to them. As for the goal, it doesn't matter if it is something big and in the future or if it is as simple as losing 3 pounds or getting an A on an upcoming test. Use the questions on the following page to create an action that supports their goal and take a few minutes to encourage them to actually do it.

Be Aware: You are not responsible for their success! Your encouragement, support, and help in creating an action plan are all you need to accomplish the dare. Ultimately, their success depends on their ability to identify what is blocking them, their willingness to let go of any fears they may have, and their commitment to stop making excuses.

Due to the difficulty level of this dare, this page has been created to help ensure your success. When you have decided who you will accomplish the dare with, use the questions below to establish their desired goal, determine what value the accomplished goal would provide, identify any blocks or obstacles to their success (usually a fear or limited belief), and create an achievable action step that can get them started. Please read over the page before meeting with the person you chose. **Do not** give them the paper and instruct them to answer the questions! You are responsible for recording their answers and following any instructions that may apply.

What would you like to do or accomplish? (What is their desired goal?) _____

_____

(Be specific; state the goal clearly. Ex: I would like to bring my math grade up to a B.)

Is this a reasonable goal? (Is it possible?) Yes / No

(Note: The goal should be achievable, if it isn't...try to pick a goal that is and try to keep it centered on the same topic. Ex. If the goal is to lose 30 pounds but this seems to be a bit unreasonable, ask them to consider changing it to losing 15 pounds just for now.)

What benefits and feelings would accomplishing this goal create? _____

_____

Can you think of any excuses or reasons why you may not achieve this goal? _____

_____

(Their answer to this question will identify any fears or obstacles that might block them from their desired success. If they can't think of any, then you can skip the next question and move directly to creating an action step for them to accomplish.)

Is this excuse or reason (actually likely a fear or negative belief) absolutely true? Yes / No   If Yes, is the reason or excuse worth giving up on the goal? Or is the goal more important?

_____ Why? _____

What would be one small and simple step you can take towards achieving this goal?

_____

Is this achievable? Yes / No   How committed are you to taking this first step? _____

★★★After you have finished this process, complete the dare by spending a few minutes really encouraging them to continue taking steps towards their desired goal. Focus on the benefits and feelings the accomplishment will produce, their ability to do it, and your faith in them.

Dare 6

"**Never take a person's dignity: it is worth everything to them, and nothing to you.**"

~Frank Barron

Dare to protect and respect the reputation of others.

According to the Merriam Webster dictionary, dignity is defined as the quality or state of being worthy, honored, or esteemed. This implies that a person's dignity makes them feel worthy or deserving of certain things. If a person's dignity gives them a sense of worthiness, then its value to each individual is immeasurable and most definitely should be protected. Nobody wants to be or feel unworthy or undeserving of even the simplest things in life. Respect, forgiveness, compassion, decency, and the basic necessities of life are just a few things that all people have a right to but not all people receive. Has anyone ever said to you, "You are unworthy of my time," "You are undeserving of my forgiveness," or perhaps the most painful to hear, "You don't deserve my love!"? What if they are wrong? (and indeed they are!) Whether or not others find you worthy or deserving doesn't really matter. You are worthy none the less and all that really matters is that you know that. When you believe you are worthy or deserving of something, you are more likely to get it and are unlikely to allow others to take it from you. For example, if you value respect, respect others, and believe you are worthy of respect, you are likely to get more respect from others and you are less likely to let others disrespect you. Just for a moment, consider what life would look and feel like if we were all worthy of a second chance, forgiveness, respect, compassion, health, wealth, and Love. Truth is, we are all worthy of all good things and no one can ever take our worthiness away. People will try to take our dignity or attempt to convince us that we are unworthy but ultimately our dignity is completely in our own hands. If we really value it, we will not surrender it to others or try to steal someone else's. As the quote above states, your dignity is worth everything to you, just as other's dignity is everything to them. The emphasis of this quote is on what someone else's dignity is worth to us – nothing! You may think that stealing their dignity allows it to be added to yours or that putting them down and ruining their reputation in the eyes of others can somehow increase your worthiness – but it doesn't. In fact, it usually does just the opposite. By protecting and respecting other's dignity, we strengthen our own.

To accomplish this dare: For 2 consecutive days, protect and respect the dignity of others as you would your own. To respect other's dignity, you must refrain from saying anything negative about them. To protect other's dignity, you need to interject positive character statements when others are trying to damage a person's reputation by slandering or insulting them. Encourage someone to reclaim their dignity if you think they have lost it.

Be Aware: You may struggle with protecting the dignity of people you don't like, and it may be hard to think of a positive thing to say about them. Just try to focus on their worthiness even if you doubt it, and let compassion help you find just the right thing to say.

How much do you value your dignity? (very much / not so much / not at all)

Has your reputation ever been attacked? Yes / No If Yes, explain what happened.

_____

_____

How do you feel when someone attacks your character or tries to steal your dignity?

_____

Have you ever done or said anything that damaged someone else's dignity? Yes / No

If Yes, explain what you did or said and why _____

_____

How do you think they felt about what you did or said? _____

Have you ever thought or felt that someone was unworthy or undeserving of your respect,

forgiveness, compassion, or Love? Yes / No If Yes, explain why _____

_____

It will be harder for me to (respect / protect) other's dignity. Why? _____

_____

Do you know anyone who seems to have lost their dignity? Yes / No If Yes, who is it and

what do you believe are the consequences of having no dignity? _____

_____

What could you do to encourage them to reclaim and value their dignity? _____

_____

Food for Thought: Maya Angelou taught, if you want to learn something you should teach it and if you want to get something you should give it to others. In other words, what we give to others expands within ourselves. Therefore, the best way for us to have more of what we want is to give what it is we want to others. This dare was designed to help you learn and accept your worthiness so that you can teach others about theirs. By taking a piece of someone else's dignity, do you not lose a piece of your own?

Encourage/Inspire Dare 1

For each of the 3 people, record how you accomplished the dare with them and what their response was.

1.) _____

_____

2.) _____

_____

3.) _____

_____

On which of the 3 occasions did you feel the best? Why? _____

_____

List a few qualities you admired in others but didn't believe you had as well.

_____ _____ _____ _____

Can you find any evidence of these qualities within yourself? Yes / No

If No, keep looking! If Yes, how does that make you feel? _____

_____

After reading this dare, did you pay more attention to the things others did that irritated you and considered if you have done the same thing? Yes / No

What did you learn? _____

_____

CONGRATULATIONS ON YOUR SUCCESS

ACCOMPLISHED
Encourage/Inspire Dare 2

The hardest part of accomplishing this dare was:

a.) finding 3 different people doing or saying kind things for me to acknowledge within the same day

b.) determining what virtues or qualities were creating or influencing their behavior

c.) mustering up the courage to acknowledge and encourage them

d.) deciding whether or not the action, kind words, and even the person were good enough or worthy of the acknowledgement or should be encouraged

e.) Other _____

Which of the following best explains why you chose to acknowledge those 3 events? (Circle any that are true and state your own if none listed apply)

a.) The action or kind words required courage and was perhaps something I would not have done if in the same situation.

b.) The action or kind words had a huge impact on the recipient.

c.) The action or kind words were done by someone who I wouldn't have expected that kind of behavior from. I was pleasantly surprised by it.

d.) The action or kind words exceeded what was necessary – it was overly generous, thoughtful, inspiring, selfless, or just extraordinary.

e.) The action or kind words could be anything nice – I was determined to accomplish the dare.

f.) Other _____

I noticed the kind acts and comments of others more than usual. True / False

Of all the kind acts and words I witnessed, I chose to acknowledge and encourage them about (25 / 50 / 75 / 100) percent of the time.

Who do you believe was most affected by what you said to them and how did they respond?

_____

_____

Doing this dare taught me _____

CONGRATULATIONS ON YOUR SUCCESS

ACCOMPLISHED
Encourage/Inspire Dare 3

The friend who helped me to complete the exercise was _____.

How did this friend seem to feel about answering the questions? _____
_____

The other 2 people I got to know better were _____ & _____

How did these 2 people react when you tried to learn more about them? _____
_____

Of the 3, who did you seem to know best? _____

Of the 3, who did you seem to know the least about? _____

Of the 3, who were you most comfortable talking to? _____

Of the 3, who do you think was most willing to let you get to know them better? (Who enjoyed the conversation the most?) _____

How did doing this dare make you feel? _____

What was the most interesting or shocking thing you learned and who was it about?
_____
_____

How would you feel if someone asked you these questions or showed an interest in getting to know you better? _____
_____

CONGRATULATIONS ON YOUR SUCCESS

ACCOMPLISHED
Encourage/Inspire Dare 4

Doing the A.B.L.E exercise on each scenario was (very easy / easy / not so easy / difficult)

I accomplished this dare by replacing the sympathy I felt towards _____
with empathy.   (Person's Name)

My initial sympathetic response or feeling was _____

_____

My empathetic response was:

(A) _____

_____

(B) _____

_____

(L) _____

_____

(E) _____

_____

How can replacing sympathy with empathy benefit others as well as yourself?

_____

_____

This dare taught me _____

_____

CONGRATULATIONS ON YOUR SUCCESS

ACCOMPLISHED
Encourage/Inspire Dare 5

This dare was (very difficult / somewhat difficult / not too hard / easy).

Who did you accomplish this dare on? _____

What was their desired goal? _____

This goal appeared to be (very / somewhat / not too / not at all) important to them and seemed (reasonable / unreasonable).

Did they seem to have any fears or negative beliefs blocking their success?

Yes / No If Yes, what was it? _____

_____

Was the fear true for them? Yes / No   Did you think it was true? Yes / No

Was their fear or excuse worth giving up on their goal? Yes / No

Did you manage to create a small and simple action step? Yes / No

If Yes, what was it? _____

Did they seem committed or willing to do the action step? Yes / No

How did doing this dare make you feel and what did you learn? _____

_____

_____

Next time I find myself procrastinating on a goal I want to achieve, I will

_____

CONGRATULATIONS ON YOUR SUCCESS

ACCOMPLISHED
Encourage/Inspire Dare 6

This dare was (very difficult / hard / not too hard / easy) for me.

To accomplish this dare, which did you have to put more effort and attention on: protecting people's dignity from others or respecting other's dignity myself ? (Underline your answer)

Why do you think that was harder? _____

_____

_____

Give 1 example of how you protected someone's dignity. _____

_____

Give 1 example of how you respected someone's dignity. _____

_____

What feelings came up for you when reading and doing this dare? _____

_____

What behaviors or thoughts changed as a result of doing this dare? _____

_____

Did you encourage someone who seemed to have little or no dignity to value and reclaim their dignity? Yes / No

How would finding yourself and others worthy of all good things benefit you?

_____

_____

CONGRATULATIONS ON YOUR SUCCESS

CHAPTER REVIEW

What is your favorite quote from this chapter? Why?

_____

_____

Which of the dares was the hardest? Why?

_____ because _____

_____

_____

Which of the dares was the easiest? Why?

_____ because _____

_____

_____

Which dare made you feel the best about what you had done? Why?

_____ because _____

_____

_____

Which dare do you think you will try to do most often? Why?

_____ because _____

_____

_____

Which dare did you do the most? # _____

Which dare did you do the least? # _____

Which dare was easiest to remember? # _____ hardest? # _____

Which dare had the most shocking/dramatic results? # _____ why? _____

_____

Which dare or dares did people seem to notice when you did it? _____

What did you learn about yourself and/or others through this chapter's exercises?

_____

_____

_____

_____

_____

_____

_____

Can you think of another way to dare yourself in order to test or build-up this virtue?

_____

_____

_____

_____

_____

_____

_____

_____

_____

What was fun about these exercises? _____

_____

_____

What was not so fun? _____

_____

Use these 2 pages to keep notes during the week, jot down ideas or thoughts, or to evaluate your success. Set goals to help you accomplish the dares and goals for practicing them in the future.

_____

_____

_____

_____

_____

_____

_____

_____

_____

_____

_____

_____

_____

_____

_____

_____

_____

_____

_____

_____

_____

_____

_____

"It is not because things are difficult that we do not dare; it is because we do not dare that things are difficult."

~Seneca

"If you inspire others to dream more, learn more, do more, and become more, you are a leader."

John Quincy Adams

CHAPTER 6

APPRECIATION

Appreciate: value; be grateful for.

Ungrateful: not feeling or showing gratitude; (taking things for granted).

As defined by *The Oxford illustrated Dictionary*

The Choice

Virtue: Appreciative

or

Vice: Ungrateful

The greatest two benefits of being appreciative are:

1.) _____

2.) _____

The two most detrimental consequences of being ungrateful are:

1.) _____

2.) _____

Appreciation Agreement

I, _____, understand that being appreciative is more beneficial to me than being ungrateful. Therefore, I agree to read the following chapter, answer the questions presented, complete any exercises, and attempt to accomplish as many dares as possible - as often as I can.

Signed: _____   Date: _____

APPRECIATION
Dare 1

"Appreciation can make a day, even change a life. Your willingness to put it into words is all that is necessary"
~Margaret Cousins

Dare to express appreciation to someone who does for you regularly but often goes unnoticed.

When someone gives us a gift or does something for us that they didn't have to do, telling them thank you is usually an immediate and natural response. However, when it is a person's job or responsibility to do something that benefits us, we tend to take what they do for granted or neglect to express our appreciation even if we are grateful. For instance, a policeman protects your neighborhood all year long, but do you thank them for their dedication when they pull you over to give you a speeding ticket that you deserve? Your parents can cook, clean house, and do laundry almost every day, but you might not thank them for it because you think – 'That's what parents are supposed to do!' Too often, we fail to appreciate what others do for us when we expect those things from them. That is why it is wiser to expect nothing and appreciate everything, than it is to expect everything and appreciate nothing. Truth is, people love to be, want to be, and sometimes need to be appreciated for the things they do for others even if it's required or expected of them. When someone feels appreciated for what they do, they're not only going to keep doing it but they will likely be happy to do it and will also do it very well. If someone feels like what they are doing is being taken for granted, they may be less enthusiastic about doing it, do it poorly, or may stop doing it all together. Therefore, it benefits us to acknowledge and express our appreciation regularly to the people who make our lives better or easier.

To accomplish this dare: Express your appreciation to someone, who does for you regularly, which you may have been taking for granted. You can choose to write them a note, give them a gift, or simply thank them in person. The important thing is to not only acknowledge what they do for you but also let them know why you appreciate it. So, try to use your answers to the questions on the following page when you are expressing how grateful you are to the person you choose to appreciate.

Be Aware: To really appreciate someone, it is best not to limit yourself by identifying or focusing solely on what service they provide or *what they do for you*. Sometimes, it's the things that people **don't do** or how they make you feel which deserve to be noticed and appreciated. If you appreciate people who don't: drink and drive, smoke while you're eating, embarrass you in front of others, finish your sentences, put you down, lie to you, constantly remind you of your mistakes, try to control you, talk behind your back, expose your secrets when they are mad at you, or act like they are better than you… then, don't let it go unnoticed.

TRUTH AND DARE

122

I may sometimes fail to express appreciation for the people who do for me because I <u>don't</u>
(think about it / feel comfortable / think it is important / feel appreciative / _____)

List 3 people who do for you regularly but have gone unnoticed or unappreciated:

    a.) _____   b.) _____   c.) _____

Acknowledge what each of them do for you or what service they provide.

    a.) _____

    b.) _____

    c.) _____

How do you benefit from what they do? Ask yourself "What would I lose or how would I
suffer if they weren't there, didn't do what was expected of them, or did a really poor job?"
Ex: If it weren't for garbage collectors, I'd have to carry our trash 3 blocks to a dumpster!

    a.) _____

    b.) _____

    c.) _____

What simple thing could you do to express your appreciation for each one? Ex: I could bring
the garbage collectors a bottle of cold water and thank them for the work they do.

    a.) _____

    b.) _____

    c.) _____

Do you think these people feel appreciated for what they do? Yes / No

How would you like them to feel when you do this dare? _____

Food for Thought: There are probably way more people than you think, whose work benefits
you, that go unnoticed or unappreciated. Janitors, bus drivers, teachers, garbage collectors,
police officers, parents, doctors, cashiers, stock clerks, food servers, and even your friends are
often taken for granted or feel unappreciated for the things they do. The best way to identify
what you appreciate about someone is to think about how things would be if they weren't
there, didn't do what you expected them to do, or did their job poorly.

APPRECIATION
Dare 2

"When it comes to life, the critical thing is whether you take things for granted or take them with gratitude."

~Gilbert Keith Chesterton

Dare to be grateful for the things you have by acknowledging and appreciating them daily.

There is a deeper Truth in the phrase, "You don't know what you got till it's gone," which offers an answer to the question, "Why did I lose it in the first place?" Most often the answer is: because you didn't appreciate it when you had it! The deeper Truth is: What we appreciate – appreciates and what we don't appreciate – depreciates. Are you grateful for the air-conditioner in your home when it's working right or does it have to break before you begin to appreciate it? Does someone around you have to get very sick before you think about and appreciate how healthy you are? Sometimes, the longer we have things the less we appreciate them and the easier it is to take them for granted. For example, when you get a new car you take extraordinary care of it at first but over time you begin to leave trash in it, wash it less, and rarely do maintenance on it at all. You still value having a car, but you don't appreciate the car as much as you did before; as a result, it begins to depreciate. Similarly, we value our health, home, family, friends, food, and possessions but often forget to acknowledge and appreciate them on a daily basis. Being grateful is not only about finding value in someone or something; it's also about acknowledging and appreciating their presence in our lives. We know that we shouldn't take people and things for granted, yet we often fail to understand **why** until after we experience the consequences of losing them. By taking the time to acknowledge and appreciate all the people, things, and events that make our lives better, we may actually decrease the chance of having to suffer through the loss of them.

To accomplish this dare: Find an object that fits comfortably in the palm of your hand and place it on the side of your bed. A rock, a coin, or a charm will work well. For the next 7 days you will use it to acknowledge all the people and things in your life that you are grateful for and value. Before you get out of bed in the morning and just as you get into bed at night, place the object in your hand and think about or list all the people and things you appreciate having in your life.

Be Aware: It is just as important, if not more important, to acknowledge and appreciate things you value but may not like. For example, you may not like school or your job very much but you definitely would not want to get kicked out or fired. If you value being educated and the financial means a job provides, it is important to acknowledge and appreciate them regardless of how they may make you feel. The things you complain most about provide you with a great place to start practicing being grateful.

On a scale of 1 to 10, with 1 being 'not grateful' and 10 being 'very grateful,' how would you rank your level of gratitude on a daily basis?

(Circle one)   1   2   3   4   5   6   7   8   9   10

Explain why you decided to give yourself that score. _____

_____

List 3 things that you believe you have taken for granted or neglected to be grateful for but definitely wouldn't want to lose.

  1.) _____

  2.) _____

  3.) _____

List 2 things that you have lost as a result of taking it for granted or neglecting to really appreciate it when you had it. (Examples: a cell phone...because I was flipping it and dropped it on the ground and it broke, a bike... because I left it outside over night and it got stolen, a ride to school with a friend... because I would make them wait too long in front my house for me to come out, a computer... because I didn't update my virus protection or do maintenance on it, my ideal weight... because I ate too much junk food, a good friend... because I betrayed them or took them for granted.)

  1.) _____

  2.) _____

List 4 things that you often complain about which you wouldn't want to live or be without? (Ex: siblings, job, parents, school, chores, police, government, friends, health, food, home)

_____, _____, _____, & _____

Which one would you like to be more grateful for and why? _____

_____

Food for Thought: When considering what we are grateful for, we often think of physical things that we wouldn't want to live without. However, it is just as important to be grateful for the non-physical things that make our lives better. Such as: the forgiveness of others, the loyalty of friends, our parent's patience, our teacher's dedication to her job, or the compassion of a stranger in a time of need. Whatever you would want to see more of in the world or from the people around you, appreciate that it already exists, give it out whenever you can, and expect it to appear more and more as a result of your efforts.

APPRECIATION
Dare 3

"If you don't appreciate it, you don't deserve it."

~ Terry Josephson

Dare to appreciate the things you have by taking care of them.

Imagine that it's a few days before your birthday and a couple of friends have just come by to take you to a movie. As you are walking out, your grandmother is walking in and she hands you a birthday card. You quickly open the card and find a 100 dollar bill inside. After thanking her for being so generous, you run back to your room and reach behind your nightstand to grab a lock box. Then you head to your closet where you keep the key to the box in the pocket of a jacket that is hanging way in the back. You open the box and place the bill neatly on top the rest of your money. You lock the box up, put it back behind the nightstand, return the key to the pocket of the jacket, shut the door to your room, and then head out the door with your friends. Why did you go through all that trouble to put the money away where it belongs instead of just throwing it on your nightstand till later? Maybe the first thought that popped into your head just now was "Because I don't want anyone to steal it!" Actually, the real reason probably has more to do with how you feel about the money, even if you do think someone in your family would steal it while you were gone. Truth is, how you treat the things you have reflects how you feel about them. When you appreciate or value something, (like money, electrical devices, card collections, or musical instruments) you are more likely to keep it where it belongs, be very protective over it, and handle it with care. When things are less important to you, (like old toys, games, books, or household items) you are less concerned with where they are, how rough you are with them, or how to care for them. So, there are things that we value and take care of and there are things that we don't value or take care of. Unfortunately, there are also things that we <u>do value</u> but <u>do not appreciate</u> or take care of because we **take them for granted.** We value our home but we don't keep it clean or do maintenance as often as we could. We value our teeth but neglect to get check-ups or brush them as often as we should. We love our computer but fail to do security upgrades and delete programs we don't need. Furniture, appliances, cars, cell phones, and clothes are also things that we may value, but you couldn't tell by the way we treat them.

To accomplish this dare: Identify at least 2 things that you really do value but you don't appreciate or care for as well as you should. For one week, treat those things as if they were the most important things you have. Every time you touch it, think about it, or use it... remember – If you don't appreciate it, you don't deserve it. If you appreciate your room, keep it clean for a week. If you appreciate your clothes, clean your closet or organize your dresser drawers during the week. If you appreciate having a microwave to heat up your food, clean it or remember to cover your food with a napkin so it won't make such a mess.

List 2 things you value and appreciate so much that you are always very careful with them, keep them where they belong, and protect them as best as you can.

_____ and _____

List 4 things that you value, but do not appreciate or take good care of because you may be taking them for granted.

1.) _____   2.) _____

3.) _____   4.) _____

How would you feel or what would be different if you didn't have each of those things.

1.) _____

2.) _____

3.) _____

4.) _____

State how you could treat each of those things better or what you should do differently.

1.) _____

2.) _____

3.) _____

4.) _____

When I don't value or appreciate something anymore, I usually (vandalize or destroy it / give it away to someone who could use it / let it sit there / get a new one / _____)

One benefit that will come from taking care of the things I value and appreciate would be

_____

The reason I sometimes don't take care of the things I value is because (I just don't think about it / I am lazy / I take them for granted / they don't belong to me / _____)

Food for Thought: As the amount of things you have increases, the likelihood of you being able to appreciate them all usually decreases. The more you have → the less you value. You may find that it is better to have fewer things that you value and care for than it would to have too many things that you do not appreciate and treat poorly.

Dare 4

"The way you cut your meat reflects the way you live." ~Confucius

Dare to appreciate the basic necessities of life.

There are certain things that our bodies need to survive, like: food, water, shelter, and air. Although the majority of people have these basic things, there are many people in the world who don't. For this reason, we should not take these things for granted. To function well on a daily basis, we also need to rest, bathe, and exercise. Again, the majority of people are able to sleep, bathe, and exercise every day and appreciate that they hardly ever have to go a day without. However, appreciating what you have is not just about being grateful that you don't have to do without. When we really value and appreciate the things we have, we will take the time to fully enjoy them when they are available to us. Truth is, when it comes to the basic necessities of life, we rarely take the time to mentally enjoy the physical experience of them. Instead, we rush through good meals, take quick showers, and stay up too late because we believe that there is something else more important that needs to be done. Often, we decide to 'squeeze in' our basic needs by eating in the car or sleeping in class. On really busy days, we may even go without eating, bathing, or sleeping. If you are hoping to 'make' time or trying to 'find' time for the basic needs of life, you are not likely appreciating or enjoying life much at all. 'Taking' the time to appreciate the things your body needs is far easier than 'losing' the time you will waste dealing with the consequences if you don't. For example, if you can't take the time to eat – you may have to make the time to be sick. If you haven't taken the time to rest or sleep – you will likely struggle to find the energy to get things done and work twice as hard doing them. If you are too busy to take a bath or shower – you can expect to have an unfavorable odor. It is important to remember the simple reason why these bodily needs are called the basic necessities of life – We need them to Live.

To accomplish this dare: Complete at least 3 of the following exercises.

1.) For 3 meals, appreciate your food by taking the time to chew it, taste it, savor it, and acknowledge how it nourishes the body and supplies it with the energy you need to live.
2.) For 2 consecutive days, give your body the recommended daily amount of water it needs – plus some. Also, try to give up sodas during these 2 days.
3.) Take 3 deep breaths of fresh air 7 times throughout the day for 2 days. Slowly breathe in through your nose…hold for at least 3 seconds and exhale slowly through your mouth. ★★★This will be the hardest to accomplish but has the greatest physical benefits!
4.) Get at least 8 hours of consecutive sleep at least 2 times in one week.

5.) Begin 3 days with 2 minutes of stretching before rushing into your day.

6.) Use an exfoliating sponge and moisturizing soap in a hot bath or shower to open your pores and allow your skin to breathe on 2 different occasions within a span of 2 weeks.

Use "N" for Never, "R" for Rarely, "S" for Sometimes, "O" for Often, and "A" for Always to identify behaviors which are keeping you from appreciating the basic necessities of life.

I _____ talk through my meal

I _____ drink more sodas or flavored drinks than water

I _____ sleep less than 7 hours a night

I _____ rush through or skip a bath or shower

I _____ multi-task while eating

I _____ neglect to stretch my muscles daily

I _____ rush through meals or eat too fast

I _____ drink only when I am thirsty

I _____ forget to take slow deep breaths regularly

I _____ eat on the go

I _____ waste food

I _____ swallow large pieces of food

I _____ skip meals

I _____ over-indulge in junk food

List one benefit for each of the following:

Taking the time to enjoy a good meal by eating slowly and being focused on the food.

Benefit: _____

Drinking enough water throughout the day to exceed the daily recommended amount.

Benefit: _____

Taking deep breaths in and slow breaths out regularly throughout the day.

Benefit: _____

Getting a good night sleep - preferably 7-8 hours.

Benefit: _____

Doing some kind of stretching or cardiovascular exercises daily.

Benefit: _____

Opening the pores of your skin by exfoliating away the dead skin once a week.

Benefit: _____

Which of these 6 exercises will be most difficult for you and why? _____

APPRECIATION
Dare 5

"One touch of Nature makes the whole world kin."   ~William Shakespeare

"Human nature is just about the only nature some people experience."

~Abigail Charleson

Dare to appreciate nature by taking the time to Be in it and learn from it.

The word nature refers to the physical or material world and its natural conditions such as the weather – often referred to as Mother Nature. Nature can also refer to someone or something's inborn qualities or characteristics – also called Human Nature. Sadly, there is a lot of truth in the quote by Abigail Charleson above. On most days, human nature and the weather are the only kinds of nature that we really ever experience. We get up, get dressed, get in a car or bus, go to work or school for 8 hours, go home, eat dinner, watch TV, take a bath, and go to sleep so we can get up tomorrow and do it all over again. Within that day, our feet never felt the grass, we didn't hear the birds singing just outside the window, the fragrance of the flowers went undetected, the warmth of the sun was not felt on our skin, and we may have even cursed the wind or the rain for messing up our hair. We tend to put more thought and energy into dealing with or protecting ourselves from nature than we do really appreciating it or being in it. Truth is, Nature has a lot to offer us both physically and mentally. Galileo, the father of Modern Science, once said, "The sun, with all those planets revolving around it and dependent on it, can still ripen a bunch of grapes as if it had nothing else in the universe to do." We often forget or fail to recognize how nature and the weather benefit us physically by supporting the needs of our body. As for the mental benefits of nature, Einstein believed that if we look more deeply into nature we will come to understand everything better. By planting a tree and watching it grow – we learn about patience. If we study how grass grows, we will learn about persistence. Nature can teach us why an 'eagle's perspective' is so valuable and what makes an owl so wise. Just imagine how different our world would be if we all learned about loyalty and the importance of community from the ever-so-small ant.

To accomplish this dare: Take the time to be in nature so you can appreciate it and learn from it. Select 4 actions (from the list on the following page) that you can do within a week's time and which you believe will help you to appreciate being in nature the most. To encourage others to also appreciate the beauty and peace that Nature has to offer, try to get someone to join you in doing at least 1 of the actions. Then, complete the "What I Could Learn From Nature" exercise.

Below is a list of a few simple ways you can appreciate nature by taking the time to actually BE in it. Fill in the blank with the letter that best represents how often you do each action. Use "N" for Never, "R" for Rarely, "S" for Sometimes, and "F" for Frequently.

_____	Have a picnic in the yard or park	_____	Go for a long bike ride
_____	Gaze at the stars in the evening sky	_____	Listen to birds singing in the morning
_____	Dance or play in the rain	_____	Roast marshmallows over a camp fire
_____	Visit a zoo	_____	Watch the sun rise or set
_____	Go on a nature hike or long walk	_____	Fly a kite in the wind
_____	Look for animal shapes in the clouds	_____	Go fishing early in the morning
_____	Sit on a beach watching the waves	_____	Let yourself get drenched by the rain
_____	Lay in the grass and admire the sky	_____	Sleep outside in a tent
_____	Play in the sand or snow	_____	Hand feed ducks some bread
_____	Walk around outside - barefooted	_____	Enjoy swinging at a playground
_____	Work in a garden	_____	Enjoy the smell of fresh flowers

From the list above, circle 4 actions you might choose to accomplish this dare. What feeling/feelings do you hope to achieve by doing these actions? (Ex: Peace, fun, awe, relaxation, closeness to others, closeness to nature/animals) _____

_____

What I Can Learn From Nature Exercise – Complete each sentence and try to find the best answer for each of the following questions.

Gazing up at the stars in the evening sky makes me feel _____

How is a planet visibly different from star? _____

Watching a beautiful sunrise or sunset makes me feel _____

How long can a sunrise or sunset last? _____

Laying down and watching the clouds on a pretty day makes me feel _____

What makes a cloud change its shape? _____

Sitting quietly in the morning listening to the birds makes me feel _____

(Male / Female) birds are more often colorful? _____ Which is often more vocal? _____

Food for Thought: As young children, we love being outside and nothing about nature really scares us. We will hold lizards and frogs in our hands, play in puddles or flood waters, and even enjoy the feel of wet mud squishing between our toes. As we get older, we spend less time connecting with nature and often need a vacation to remind us how much we love being in it. Is it possible that one reason we become more stressed as we get older is because we disconnect from nature and the playfulness it offered us as children?

APPRECIATION
Dare 6

"Nothing is so beautiful, that under certain conditions it will not look ugly."
~Oscar Wilde

"Life is a mirror-It will reflect back to the thinker what he thinks into it."
~Ernest Holmes

Dare to seek out the beauty or positive in things which appear ugly or negative.

You're probably familiar with the phrase – Beauty is in the eye of the beholder. What you may think is beautiful, someone else may find to be disgusting or ugly. For the most part, many people will agree that a rainbow after a storm is beautiful. As is, the ocean on a warm summer day or a snow capped mountain-view from a cozy cabin. However, when it comes to people, situations, and the circumstances of our lives – what we see and how we perceive or judge them is completely subjective and unique. You may think I am rich and I can think I am poor. You may see me as thin and I may view myself as fat. You may think that my boyfriend/girlfriend breaking up with me is a great thing and I may see it as the end of the world. I can believe that a weed ruins a garden; yet, James Russell Lowell believes that "A weed is no more than a flower in disguise." Confucius, a great philosopher, stated that "Everything has beauty, but not everyone sees it." Although it may seem impossible to believe, there is beauty to be found in world hunger, natural disasters, war, poverty, disease, crime, and even death. On a more personal level, we will not likely find beauty in emotional pain, physical or mental abuse, neglect, rejection, lack, and loss (while we are experiencing it or after) if we aren't looking for it. Sometimes, we will see the beauty of our struggles or 'negative' circumstances much later or after the pain is gone. Truth is, <u>Everything that happens 'to' us – happens 'for' us</u>. In the words of Gandhi, "Our greatest struggles develop our greatest strengths." What we perceive as negative or ugly life experiences are better if viewed as opportunities to learn, grow, and create positive changes. We need only to look for the good or beauty in a person, thing, or event - in order to find it!

<u>To accomplish this dare:</u> Practice appreciating the events and people you perceive as negative by seeking out the good or positive experiences or lessons they may have to offer. Complete the "Find the Good in Everything" exercise on the following page and practice asking yourself – "What can I learn or what good can come from this?" Try to identify which virtue each negative experience is trying to develop or strengthen. Ex. If a friend betrays me, I have an opportunity to practice forgiveness and loyalty. If my mom ruins my plans for the weekend, my ability to be accepting and respectful will likely be tested.

Give 2 examples from your personal experiences that support the phrase – Beauty is in the eye of the beholder. (One where you thought something/someone was beautiful but others disagreed and one where you found it difficult to find beauty where others did find it.)

1.) I believe _____ is beautiful, but _____ disagrees.

2.) _____ thinks _____ is beautiful, but I don't see it.

Find the Good in Everything – Exercise

1.) Find something beautiful about 2 animals that most people would agree are ugly.

What is beautiful about a _____ is _____

What is beautiful about a _____ is _____

2.) Find something positive about someone who usually has a negative effect on you or who you have a very negative opinion of.

One positive thing about _____ is _____

3.) Find 2 events from the past that you once viewed as negative but now you can see the good that came from them.

I thought it was horrible when _____

but it actually was good because _____.

I was really hurt or upset when _____ but

I am glad it happened because _____.

4.) Consider what positive result could come from a current event or circumstance that you consider negative.

I don't see anything beautiful or positive about _____

_____ yet, but one positive result that may come from it is _____

_____

5.) Explore what good could come from what burdens you the most in life.

I really struggle with or am burdened by _____

But the good that can come from it is _____

ACCOMPLISHED
Appreciation Dare 1

Who did you choose to express your appreciation to, and why? _____

_____

How did you choose to express your appreciation? What did you do and say?

_____

_____

How did the person respond when you expressed your appreciation for them?

_____

I felt _____ before doing the dare, _____ when I

was doing the dare and _____ after I did the dare.

What is one important thing you learned about appreciation from this dare?

_____

_____

When it comes to appreciating people, (Mark T for True and F for False)

_____ I appreciate the people who do for me and regularly express it.

_____ I sometimes take people for granted.

_____ I often expect things from people that I should be appreciating.

_____ I enjoy expressing my appreciation for others.

_____ It is important to me that people know I appreciate them and that I don't take them for granted.

_____ I believe people know I appreciate them and I don't need to tell them

_____ I might need to practice acknowledging and expressing what I appreciate about others on a more regular basis.

_____ I think we should expect certain things from people and that we shouldn't have to appreciate everything good they do for us.

CONGRATULATIONS ON YOUR SUCCESS

Appreciation Dare 2

What object did you use as a gratitude reminder? _____

Where did you keep it? _____

Was it easier to do the exercise in the morning or at night? _____
Why? _____

How did acknowledging what you were grateful for daily make you feel?

_____

It was (very easy / somewhat easy / somewhat hard / very hard) to appreciate or be grateful for things I do not like experiencing or having but value what they give me.

The 5 things I seem to be most grateful for are: 1. _____

2. _____ 3. _____

4. _____ 5. _____

What did you learn from this dare about gratitude and appreciation? Or what do you think is the most important thing to remember from what you read?

_____

_____

What do you think is the greatest benefit of practicing gratitude? _____

_____

Will you keep your gratitude rock and continue to acknowledge daily what you are grateful for? YES / NO

CONGRATULATIONS ON YOUR SUCCESS

ACCOMPLISHED
Appreciation Dare 3

What 2 things did you choose to treat better or take care of for a week?

_____ and _____

How did you treat them differently? What did you do to care for them better?

1.) _____

2.) _____

The one thing I think I take for granted and mistreat more than anything else,

would have to be _____

This dare helped me realize that I want to appreciate and take better care of

_____ because _____

I would rather have: (Underline your most honest answer)

(more things that I appreciate less or less things that I appreciate more).

Why? _____

_____

The most difficult thing about taking care of the things we value is _____

_____ but,

the benefit is _____

What I want to remember most from this dare is _____

_____

CONGRATULATIONS ON YOUR SUCCESS

ACCOMPLISHED
Appreciation Dare 4

Which 3 exercises did you do? If you did more, which were the 3 hardest?

1.) _____

2.) _____

3.) _____

For each of the above, explain how each exercise differed from your usual behavior. For example: Taking in 3 deep breaths of air 7 times a day for 2 days is different from my usual behavior of just breathing regularly and not thinking much about it.

1.) _____

_____

2.) _____

_____

3.) _____

_____

For each exercise above, what would be the benefit of making it a habit?

1.) _____

2.) _____

3.) _____

Of the basic necessities of life, I seem to appreciate _____

the most and _____ the least.

The most important thing I learned from doing this dare was _____

_____

CONGRATULATIONS ON YOUR SUCCESS

ACCOMPLISHED
Appreciation Dare 5

What 4 actions did you choose to do in order to appreciate nature by taking the time to actually Be in it?

    1.) _____

    2.) _____

    3.) _____

    4.) _____

Describe how you felt when you were doing each of the above? Benefits?

    1.) _____

    2.) _____

    3.) _____

    4.) _____

During the week that you worked on this dare, what did you learn about nature or what new thoughts or feelings did you have about being in nature?

_____

_____

My favorite thing to do in nature is _____

_____ because _____

I want to take the time to be in nature at least (once / twice / three or more times) a week.

TRUTH AND DARE

CONGRATULATIONS ON YOUR SUCCESS

ACCOMPLISHED
Appreciation Dare 6

I found it (extremely hard / somewhat difficult / not too hard / very easy) to find something beautiful about the 2 animals most people agree to be ugly.

When it comes to people, I tend to: (Circle one)

- look more for their beauty and focus on their positive qualities.
- see their flaws and dwell on their negative qualities.

When I reflected back on 2 events from the past that were difficult for me but ended up

being good for me, I felt or learned _____

_____

I found it (extremely hard / somewhat difficult / not too hard / very easy) to consider what positive results could come from, or what I could learn from, a current event or circumstance that I considered to be negative.

What is one negative event or experience you had while trying to accomplish this dare or

perhaps are experiencing now? _____

_____

What virtue(s) could this experience develop or strengthen in you? How/Why

_____

_____

What do you believe accomplishing this dare taught you and how will you continue to

use it? _____

_____

Trying to grow and learn from my negative experiences will be beneficial to me because

_____

CONGRATULATIONS ON YOUR SUCCESS

CHAPTER REVIEW

What is your favorite quote from this chapter? Why?

_____

_____

Which of the dares was the hardest? Why?

_____ because _____

_____

_____

Which of the dares was the easiest? Why?

_____ because _____

_____

_____

Which dare made you feel the best about what you had done? Why?

_____ because _____

_____

_____

Which dare do you think you will try to do most often? Why?

_____ because _____

_____

_____

Which dare did you do the most? # _____

Which dare did you do the least? # _____

Which dare was easiest to remember? # _____ hardest? # _____

Which dare had the most shocking/dramatic results? # _____ why? _____

_____

Which dare or dares did people seem to notice when you did it? _____

What did you learn about yourself and/or others through this chapter's exercises?

_____

_____

_____

_____

_____

_____

Can you think of another way to dare yourself in order to test or build-up this virtue?

_____

_____

_____

_____

_____

_____

_____

What was fun about these exercises? _____

_____

_____

What was not so fun? _____

_____

Use these 2 pages to keep notes during the week, jot down ideas or thoughts, or to evaluate your success. Set goals to help you accomplish the dares and goals for practicing them in the future.

_____

_____

_____

_____

_____

_____

_____

_____

_____

_____

_____

_____

_____

_____

_____

_____

_____

_____

_____

_____

_____

_____

_____

_____

_____

"It is not because things are difficult that we do not dare; it is because we do not dare that things are difficult."

"As we express our gratitude, we must never forget that the highest appreciation is not to utter words, but to live by them."

John Fitzgerald Kennedy

CHAPTER 7

LOYALTY

Loyal: faithful; steadfast in allegiance. Reliable.

Disloyal: unfaithful; untrue to one's allegiance. Untrustworthy.

As defined by *The Oxford illustrated Dictionary*

The Choice

Virtue: Loyalty

or

Vice: Disloyalty

The greatest two benefits of being loyal and dependable are:

1.) _____

2.) _____

The two most detrimental consequences of being disloyal and unreliable are:

1.) _____

2.) _____

Loyalty Agreement

I, _____, understand that being loyal and dependable are more beneficial to me than being disloyal and unreliable. Therefore, I agree to read the following chapter, answer the questions presented, complete any exercises, and attempt to accomplish as many dares as possible – as often as I can.

Signed: _____   Date: _____

Dare 1

"A good word is an easy obligation; but not to speak ill requires only our silence; which costs us nothing."
~John Tilloston – Archbishop of Canterberry

"Gossip needn't be false to be evil – there is a lot of truth that shouldn't be passed around."
~ Frank A. Clark

Dare to be loyal to others by not speaking ill of anyone.

Have you ever noticed how much of our normal day to day conversations include speaking poorly about others? Unfortunately, when it comes to the negative things we say about others, it doesn't matter if it's true, false, or just an opinion …it's almost always hurtful and damaging to the person's reputation. Imagine that someone you trust has just told you 3 things about one of your classmates: 1.) They are a pretty good student, 2.) They have plenty of friends, and 3.) They were arrested for the robbery of a local convenient store. You may believe all 3, but guess which one you would be most likely to remember. Even if the person was cleared of the charges because they were actually at work when the crime was committed, the arrest is what you will likely remember the most about that person. Oddly enough, people tend to believe and remember the negative things that are said, about others or even themselves, more than they do the positive things. As unreasonable as it is, we are quick to believe the negative things that we hear, without any evidence at all, but we will question or doubt the good things even if there is evidence to support it. As a result, getting someone to believe something negative about themselves and/or others is far too easy; trying to get them to forget may be almost impossible. Truth is, avoiding speaking poorly about a friend defines you as a great friend; refusing to speak ill of anyone defines you as a great person. In her quote, "Great minds discuss ideas. Average minds discuss events. Small minds discuss people," Eleanor Roosevelt defines what makes for the most valuable conversations and exposes what kinds of people are most likely to be having them.

To accomplish this dare: Make it through an entire day without saying anything negative about anyone. This dare may be a lot harder than you think because talking negatively about others is done so regularly and often without any thought. You will have to be very observant of what you say throughout the day in order to assure you have not slipped up. So, it might be helpful to practice doing it for only an hour here and there for a few days before you attempt to make it through a whole day. You might even want to let others know what you are doing so they can help monitor what you say.

Be Aware: Some people really enjoy spending most of their time talking about others. Being around them will make this dare tough but if you are one of them it will be even tougher. Try talking about events and ideas to avoid the topic of people. If you have to talk about people, make sure what you say is positive.

What thoughts or feelings came up when reading this dare? _____

_____

Accomplishing this dare will be (very easy / somewhat easy / somewhat hard / very hard).

Most of my day to day conversations revolve around (people / events / ideas / _____)

What I enjoy talking about most would be _____.

When I do talk about people, it is more often (positive / negative).

When someone tells me something positive about someone, I will usually:

    a.) Take their word for it

    b.) Ask for evidence

    c.) Doubt it

    d.) _____

When someone tells me something negative about someone, I will usually:

    a.) Take their word for it

    b.) Ask for evidence

    c.) Doubt it

    d.) _____

What I remember most about people are the (positive / negative) things they have done.

Of all the people I know, _____ is the person who spends the most time talking negatively about others. How do you think this behavior effects their relationships or what effect does it have on their reputation/character?

_____

_____

Someone I rarely hear talking negative about other people would be _____.

How does their behavior effect their reputation? _____

_____

Food for Thought: Sir Winston Churchill once said, "By swallowing evil words unsaid, no one has ever harmed his stomach." In other words, choosing to keep your negative opinions about others to yourself will **not** make you sick. Did you notice that the authors of both this quote and the quote from the previous page chose the word 'evil' to describe gossip and negative comments? What they are both emphasizing with their word choice is that nothing 'good' can come from saying things that can damage someone's reputation.

Dare 2

"Promises may fit the friends, but non-performance will turn them into enemies."
~Ben Franklin

Dare to be loyal to your friends by being the kind of friend who never becomes an enemy.

When people get married they exchange vows and make a promise to be there for each other through the good times and the bad... "Until death do us part." As you know, many marriages die long before the people do and the end result is often a relationship filled with anger, resentment, bitterness, and regret. When a friendship begins, there are many unspoken promises. We promise to be a loyal, honest, empathetic, forgiving, and trustworthy friend and expect our friend will be this way too. These promises are fairly easy to keep during good times but are much more challenging during the tough times. Truth is, being a friend is not solely defined by what you do together in good times; more importantly, being a friend is about who and where you are when times are tough. Even simple things like standing up for a friend, being honest with a friend, or just being willing to listen to a friend who really needs to talk can sometimes require more loyalty and courage than even a good friend can muster up. Being loyal to a friend 'until the end' defines you as a great friend. Yet, the best kind of friend to have, and to be, is a friend who is a friend even *past* 'the end.' You probably already know that when promises are broken or trust is betrayed, great friends can quickly become worst enemies. In fact, an ex-best friend makes a horrible enemy because they know exactly what to say and do to hurt you. Sadly, when best friends get into a fight, loyalty is frequently the first thing to go. All too often, when we feel betrayed or rejected by our friends, we let our feelings direct our behaviors, instead of our hearts or morals. We may talk poorly about them, point out all their flaws, attack their emotional weak spots, and/or expose all their secrets without even giving it a second thought. By choosing to continue 'being' a friend even past 'the end' and refusing to act like or become an enemy, you prove yourself to be not only a great friend but also define yourself as a great person.

To accomplish this dare: Within the next 7 days, attempt to accomplish all 5 of the challenges on the following page. Numbers 1, 3 and 5 should be rather easy to do and you should try to accomplish each of those at least 3 times during the week. Numbers 2 and 4 may be a bit more difficult but you should be able to find at least one opportunity during the week to accomplish these challenges. Each night, record on loose leaf or in an old notebook whether you succeeded at being a friend or whether you acted more like an enemy when the challenges presented themselves to you. If any of the challenges do not present themselves within the 7 days, you may use a memory or past experience to accomplish the dare.

1.) Be loyal to your friends by standing up for them when others are talking poorly about them. Change the focus of the conversation by exposing their good qualities and emphasizing how much you value their friendship.

2.) Be honest with a friend by exposing a <u>truth</u> that they may be denying or ignoring even though you are afraid it might hurt them or that they may have a negative reaction. Ex. A friend is mad because they found out someone was talking behind their back and they say, "I would never do that to them; I can't believe they did this to me!" Yet, you know that your friend has talked behind that person's back in a negative way many times before. You could respond, "Well, in all honesty, you **have** done that to them."

3.) Be empathetic with your friends by acknowledging and validating their feelings instead of focusing only on the details of the situation or possible solutions. When people we care about are angry, hurt, or stressed, we often focus on trying to fix things for them by throwing out solutions or by taking actions to change the current conditions. However, it is very important to first acknowledge and validate their feelings. You can do this by using sentences like, "I understand how you feel and I am sorry you are hurting," or "It is perfectly understandable that you feel the way you do in this situation." Sometimes, empathy and validation are all they really wanted and the solution was already clear to them.

4.) Be forgiving with your friends by inquiring about their thoughts that lead to the behavior that hurt you. It is hard to forgive a friend if you believe they have 'intentionally' done something to hurt or betray you. Truth is, your friend's behavior may have had nothing to do with you and was never intended to be an attack on you at all even though you were hurt by it. Learning that they never meant to hurt you can make it easier to forgive them and strengthen the friendship. If they did mean to hurt you, it is likely a response to being hurt BY you. In this case, learning that their attack is actually a defensive response can help you to be more understanding and offer you the opportunity to clarify your actions and apologize if necessary. Then, if you are still finding it hard to forgive them or remain their friend, refuse to become an enemy by resisting revenge or counter attack.

5.) Be trustworthy. Keep all personal information confidential – no matter what! Don't share with others what you know about your friend if it's something they told you in confidence or if it's something that may hurt them if it is revealed. If in doubt… don't shout it out!

Circle the challenge that you believe will be the hardest for you to do. #1 #2 #3 #4 #5

Circle the challenge that you do most often. #1 #2 #3 #4 #5

Circle the challenge you would most want a friend to do for you. #1 #2 #3 #4 #5

Dare 3

"You cannot escape the responsibilities of tomorrow by evading it today."

~Abraham Lincoln

Dare to be loyal to your responsibilities by avoiding procrastination.

Have you ever procrastinated (put off) studying for a test or writing a paper till the night before it was due? Have you ever waited till you got yelled at to do your chores or submitted a poorly done project for school because you waited too long to begin working on it? If you are like most people, you probably answered with a sighing – Yes! You may have realized by now that procrastination is easy in the beginning - but recovering from it can be very painful and exhausting. A contemporary writer named Olin Miller sums up the consequences of procrastination best in his quote, "If you want to make an easy job seem mighty hard, just keep putting off doing it." Truth is, procrastination is a self-defeating and self-sabotaging habit that not only makes our tasks more difficult and costly, but it can also keep us from achieving our goals altogether. Waiting for the last minute to study for a test or write a paper often creates plenty of unwanted and unnecessary stress and results in an undesirable grade. So why do it? Like the quote from Olin Miller explains, an easy job – like filling up your car with gas – can become mighty hard if you procrastinate so long that you end up having to push it to the next gas station. Putting off paying the bills can cost you late fees or your services can be shut off. People even put off going to the doctor when they are sick because they are too busy. Is this not self-defeating and irrational? The best way to avoid procrastination is to identify the goal or desired result, determine what actions are required or should be taken in order to get the best result, acknowledge the benefits of not putting off the necessary actions required to succeed, and expose the negative consequences that waiting till later will likely produce. Focusing on the feelings you will have when your to-do-list is – DONE can also help to motivate you into action!

To accomplish this dare: Use the questions on the following page to help you discover where procrastination may be blocking your success or creating undesirable results. Choose 1 goal that you desire to accomplish and complete the "Procrastinator Eliminator" exercise on the bottom of the page. Then, take at least one of the action steps towards achieving the goal.

Be Aware: Procrastination is not always a sign of laziness. For this reason, it is good to seriously consider or question yourself about **why** you may be procrastinating. If you are procrastinating with something you really want to do…Fear is likely the cause. Fear of success, fear of failure, fear of not being worthy of the results and fear of 'what's next' are all capable of keeping you from accomplishing what you desire by creating the habit of procrastination.

When it comes to studying, I will usually:

    a.) Read, practice, or review the material daily and begin studying days in advance

    b.) Wait until a few days before the test and try to study a little each night

    c.) Procrastinate until the night before and then cram as much in as possible

    d.) _____

When it comes to my household chores/responsibilities, I will usually:

    a.) Do them when I am supposed to or when I see they need to be done

    b.) Wait until I am told to do them or until they can't be put off any longer

    c.) Procrastinate so long that someone else has to do it and I get in trouble

    d.) _____

What are 2 responsibilities that you **do not like** to do and often try to 'put off' doing them?

    1.) I sometimes put off _____ and the most common negative

    consequence or result of my procrastination is _____

    2.) I sometimes put off _____ and the most common negative

    consequence or result of my procrastination is _____

One thing that I would like to do is _____ but I

have not given it much time or effort because _____

I believe that I may be putting off _____ because of my

fear of _____

Procrastinator Eliminator

Identify Goal: _____

Action Steps: What are 2 simple things you can do that will move you closer to that goal?

    1.) _____

    2.) _____

What are some benefits that can come from taking these actions steps now? _____

_____

What results or consequences would you expect to get by choosing to procrastinate?

_____

Dare 4

"**The reward for conformity is that everyone likes you but yourself.**"

~Rita Mae Brown

Dare to be loyal to yourself by avoiding peer pressure and social conformity.

In order to avoid conflict, criticism, or possible rejection, we often allow the majority to determine our behaviors instead of our conscience. We are taught that it is better to 'Go with the flow,' than it is to 'make waves.' We grow up hearing and believing 'if you stick out, you're like a sore thumb' and 'the majority is always right.' For the purpose of this dare, we will define peer pressure and social conformity like this:

Peer Pressure is doing something you don't want to do - so not to be left out.

Social Conformity is not doing something you want to do - in order to fit in.

Let's use the old Chinese Proverb, "One dog barks at something and a hundred bark at the bark," to better understand peer pressure. When one dog in a kennel barks at something, all the other dogs begin barking as well. They may not know what or who they are barking at, but why is simple - because 'everyone else is doing it.' Barking at the bark is an example of peer pressure. When reason would have you do one thing but a majority influences you to do the opposite – you have given in to peer pressure. The old Chinese Proverb, "The bird that flies out of its flock is the first one targeted by hunters" explains why social conformity is so popular; it's risky and takes a lot of courage to fly out on your own or to be different from the rest. When you refrain from doing what you want to do because the majority or society convinces you that you shouldn't – this is social conformity. With peer pressure, what you DO (barking at the bark) goes against what you THINK you should WANT to do (find out what the barking is about). With social conformity, what you WANT to do (fly out own your own) goes against what you THINK you should DO (stay where it is safe with the flock). Truth is, giving into peer pressure goes against Who We Are and social conformity keeps us from Who We Want to Be.

To accomplish this dare: First, complete the 2 exercises on the following page. Then, be loyal to yourself by refusing to DO any 2 from the "Peer Pressure Exercise" for 3 days in a row and DON'T DO any 1 from the "Social Conformity Exercise" for an entire week.

Be Aware: Avoiding social conformity is NOT about being rebellious and breaking rules or laws that exist for our own good. Avoiding social conformity is about:

1.) Forming your opinions and beliefs based off of your own personal experiences, feelings, and reasoning.
2.) Valuing Who You Are more than what others think of you.
3.) Having the courage to express your opinion and beliefs without fear of criticism or rejection.

"Peer Pressure Exercise"

Use a check to indicate which of the following actions have you felt 'pressured' into doing. Use the extra blanks to list any other things you may have felt pressured to do.

_____ Lying _____ Cheating _____ Cursing _____ Bullying _____ Stealing

_____ Going somewhere I didn't want to go _____ Talking behind a friend's back

_____ Having Sex _____ Taking Drugs _____ Drinking Alcohol _____ Smoking

_____ Being disrespectful _____ Gossiping _____ Vandalizing _____ Bragging

_____ Quitting something _____ Dressing provocatively _____ Changing my look/style

_____ Keeping my thoughts/opinions to myself _____ Agreeing when I really disagree

_____ _____ _____

When I have or do give into peer pressure, the reason is most often because I am trying to

(avoid criticism / prevent conflict / gain other's approval / fit in / _____)

"Social Conformity Exercise"

Try to complete the following sentence using each of the topics listed. A completed sentence will look like this… When it comes to _expressing my feelings_, my friends would say I shouldn't _be so honest_ but I want to _always let others know how I really feel_.

Topics: Clothes / Food / Religion / My relationships / My body image / My personality / Music / Television / Sex / School / My goals / My future career / Love / Personal hygiene

When it comes to _____, (society / my parents / my friends / _____)

would say I shouldn't _____ but

I want to _____

I seem to conform the most when it comes to pleasing (society / my parents / my friends).

When it comes to the topic of _____ I almost **always** conform to the

majority because _____.

When it comes to the topic of _____ I almost **never** conform to the

majority because _____.

Dare 5

"The only way to have a friend is to Be one." ~Ralph Waldo Emerson

Dare to be the kind of friend that you would want to have.

As the quote above suggest, friendships can often be one-sided or unbalanced relationships in which only one person really receives the benefits. This is because there seems to be more people eager to have a friend than there are people who are actually willing to 'be' one. Truth is, many friendships don't last because we expect our friends to 'be' what we are unable to 'be' ourselves. We expect them to be loyal to us by not talking behind our backs, yet we talk behind theirs. We expect them to be trustworthy, honest, sympathetic, dependable, and forgiving - even when we are not. In other words, we want them to **be** a better friend to us than we are willing to be to them. Although most people enjoy having a friend when they need one, many often disappear when it is time to actually 'be' one. To have a friend and to be a friend requires a real, yet simple, understanding of what a friend is! Henry Ford does a great job of defining what a friend is in his quote, "My best friends are the ones who bring out the best in me." It's that simple! You know you have a real friend when that person always seems to bring out the best in you and you know you are a real friend if you are always trying to bring out the best in another. In friendship there is no competition, judgments, or 'unrealistic expectations' to keep you from always being good to one another and wanting the best for each other. In his quote, "When we seek to discover the best in others, we somehow bring about the best in ourselves," William Arthur Ward exposes one of the greatest benefits of being a good friend – becoming a better person.

To accomplish this dare: Explore what kind of friend you are by responding honestly to the statements on the following page. Then, on a separate piece of paper with a heading of "The Kind of Friend I Aim to BE," complete the 7 if/then statements provided to expose what you believe true friendship is and define the kind of friend you want to be to others. It doesn't matter if you write it like a letter or just copy and type the sentences as they are with your responses added to them. Feel free to add to it or change anything you disagree with. Share your paper with at least 1 person who you can trust will help you Be the kind of friend you aim to BE.

Be Aware: You may define a friend as someone who does this or who shouldn't do that, but this puts expectations and demands on the friendship that will ultimately cause disappointment and can destroy the relationship. Like Love, friendships are not always like a two-way street with both sides giving and receiving equally. The best thing you can do for a friend, as well as for yourself, is to be more concerned with what your side of the street looks like and let you friend be concerned with their own side.

Explore What Kind of Friend You Are

Respond to each statement below with one of the following:
AT (Always True), MT (Mostly True), ST (Sometimes True), RT (Rarely True)

_____ I love being there for a friend when they need my help or just want me to listen.

_____ I encourage my friends by letting them know how much I believe in them and their ability to accomplish whatever goals they may have.

_____ I inspire my friends by complimenting their good qualities and their achievements.

_____ I accept my friends as they are. I avoid trying to change them through force or fear.

_____ I refrain from judging or putting demands on my friends by accepting the Truth that we may not value the same qualities or share the same opinions or behaviors.

_____ I am true and loyal to my friends even when they are not true and loyal to me.

_____ I wish for my friends all the things I would want for myself and do not feel threatened by their success even when it exceeds my own.

"The Kind of Friend I Aim to BE"

(Use the sentences above as a guide for completing the following if you have trouble)

If being a friend is not defined by what you do together during good times; but rather by who and where you are during the tough times... Then, I want to be the kind of friend who.

_____

If encouraging someone is a great way to empower them... Then, I want to be the kind of friend that _____.

If acknowledging and complimenting a friend's good qualities and achievements will inspire them to be the best person they can be... Then, I want to be the kind of friend who

_____

because I want to help them to feel _____.

If acceptance is one of the greatest gifts I can give to a friend... Then, I want to be the kind of friend who _____.

I want my friends to know that they are _____.

If respecting my friend's opinions, values, behaviors, or qualities that differ from mine can strengthen the friendship... Then, I want to be the kind of friend who would NOT _____ when my friends and I disagree.

If friends are like the bank vaults where we can keep all our valuables and secrets safe...

Then, I want to be the kind of friend who _____

and who will never _____ even in the biggest fight or if the friendship ends.

If wishing the best for others, reveals the best within ourselves... Then, I want to be the kind of friend who wishes for my friends all the _____, _____,

_____, & _____ they desire and deserve – Plus MORE!.

Dare 6

"I do the very best I know how – the very best I can; and I mean to keep on doing so until the very end."

~Abraham Lincoln

Dare to be loyal to yourself by always doing your best.

Have you ever done anything halfway or started something that you never finished? For the most part, our intentions are usually to do our best at whatever it is we do. Yet, our actions often end up being 'less than our best.' Unfortunately, we are commonly judged on the results of our actions and not our intentions. When we don't do our best, others may judge what we did do as if it were our best even when it wasn't, and we will judge ourselves because we know we could have done better. To do our best requires us to BE 3 things: Clear, Confident, and Committed. Sometimes we fail to do our best because we are not clear about what our best would be or we lose focus of our goal. Henry Ford stated, "Obstacles are those frightful things you see when you take your eyes off your goals." Being clear and focused on what you want to achieve and why, will motivate you to do your best to accomplish it and can help you to avoid doing 'less than your best' when obstacles present themselves. However, being clear of what you want is not enough because that only serves to create your best intention. John Eliot sums up the key to doing your best in his quote, "To be a top performer you have to be passionately committed to what you're doing and insanely confident about your ability to pull it off." It is very important to know that you are capable of accomplishing your goal. Being confident in your ability to do something is what makes it possible. In the moment you stop believing you can – you confirm you won't. Although not being clear and confident often keeps us **doing** 'less than our best' – not being committed to always doing our best is what keeps us **being** - 'less than our best.' Truth is, being willing and committed to always doing our best is far more important than what we achieve or fail to achieve. In other words, "It doesn't matter if you win or lose… it's how you play the game." By committing to **DOING** nothing less than your best…you always achieve **BEING** your best.

To accomplish this dare: Choose 2 topics, from the box on the following page, that you may be doing 'less than your best' with and use them to complete the "Clear and Confident" exercise. A 3rd topic (the Truth And Dare program) has been chosen for you to complete as well. Commit to doing your best with at least 2 of the topics for 3 consecutive days. If you like, you may choose to substitute one of the topics with a goal you have not accomplished yet or would like to start working on.

Be Aware: Your best is never going to be the same from one moment to the next because everything is changing all the time. What may be your best in one moment may not be possible in the next because other factors have influenced your best into something less. If you normally run a mile a day but you run less when you are sick – you still did your best!

Eating Healthy	Doing Chores	Homework	Studying	Good Hygiene
Positive Thinking	Being Respectful		Complimenting Others	Exercising
Being Generous	Being a Loyal Friend		Forgiveness	Living in the NOW
Encouraging Others	Being Authentic	Honesty		Being Accepting of Others
Being Grateful	Loving Myself		Truth And Dare Program (Mandatory)	

Clear and Confident Exercise

Use any 2 topics (plus the mandatory topic) to complete the exercise.

Topic 1 - I may be doing 'less than my best' when it comes to _____

CLEAR: To do your best, <u>what</u> would you have to do and/or avoid doing and <u>why</u> would you want to? _____

_____

CONFIDENT: Use 1 sentence to explain how you <u>know</u> you can do what you wrote above.

_____

_____

Topic 2 - I may be doing 'less than my best' when it comes to _____

CLEAR: To do your best, <u>what</u> would you have to do and/or avoid doing and <u>why</u> would you want to? _____

_____

CONFIDENT: Use one sentence to explain how you <u>know</u> you can do your best.

_____

Topic 3 - I may be doing 'less than my best' when it comes to <u>the Truth And Dare Program</u>

CLEAR: To do your best, <u>what</u> would you have to do and/or avoid doing and <u>why</u> would you want to? _____

_____

CONFIDENT: Use one sentence to explain how you <u>know</u> you can do your best.

_____

ACCOMPLISHED
Loyalty Dare 1

Not speaking ill of anyone for a whole day took
(no effort / a little effort / more effort than I thought / a lot of effort)

Did anyone notice what you were doing or help monitor you? Yes / No

I accomplished this dare (less often / more often) than I thought I would.

I was (shocked / pleased / disappointed / _____) by the amount of negative things I say about people.

When other people were talking poorly about someone, this dare became (harder / easier) for me.

When doing this dare, how did you feel or respond when someone else began speaking ill of others? _____

_____

If I had to guess why people spend so much time talking poorly about people or why they enjoy putting others down, I would say it is because...

_____

_____

What did you learn from doing this dare or what do you really want to remember about it?

_____

_____

The greatest benefit of avoiding saying negative things about others is _____

_____

CONGRATULATIONS ON YOUR SUCCESS

ACCOMPLISHED
Loyalty Dare 2

Which of the 5 challenges did you find to be most difficult? # _____

Why? _____

Which challenge was the easiest to do and which needs the most practice?

Easiest was # _____ Needs the most practice is # _____

Of all the people I know, I believe that _____ is most likely the kind of friend who would remain a friend even past the end.

Whenever I have a problem or argument with a friend, I most often (remain a loyal friend / become or act more like an enemy).

Have you ever had a friend become an enemy? Yes / No If Yes, what could you do differently

if that same experience happened again today? _____

_____

_____

How committed are you to keep practicing each of the 5 challenges? Use CC for completely committed, RC for really committed, SC for somewhat committed, or UC for uncommitted.

_____ Loyalty _____ Honesty _____ Empathetic _____ Forgiving _____ Trustworthy

Which 3 would you want your friends to be most committed to? Why? _____

_____

What do you think is the greatest benefit of practicing this dare? _____

_____

CONGRATULATIONS ON YOUR SUCCESS

ACCOMPLISHED
Loyalty Dare 3

What 2 things did you acknowledge you do not like to do and often put off?

_____ and _____

Did your thinking or actions around these 2 things change? Yes / No

If yes, How? _____

List 1 negative or undesirable outcome which you recently or often experience as a result of

procrastinating. _____

_____

My procrastination seems to be driven mostly by (laziness / fear).

I accomplished this dare by identifying my goal as _____

_____ and taking the action step of _____

_____

What feelings or results did taking this action step produce? _____

_____

What feelings and results does procrastinating usually produce? _____

_____

I feel better when my responsibilities are (already / still have to be) done.

The most important thing I learned from doing this dare was _____

_____

CONGRATULATIONS ON YOUR SUCCESS

ACCOMPLISHED
Loyalty Dare 4

I accomplished this dare by refusing to be pressured into _____

and _____ for at least 3 days.

I found it (easy / a little challenging / difficult) to go against the crowd and the feelings

I experienced when I did were _____

Did you witness anyone else being pressured into something you could tell they didn't want
to do while trying to accomplish your dare? Yes / No

If yes, how did it make you feel and what, if anything, did you do or say? _____

_____

Have you ever pressured someone into doing something they didn't want to do or quickly

regretted doing? Yes / No If Yes, why and how did it make you feel? _____

_____

_____

(None / Not many / Some / Plenty / Too many) of my thoughts and actions are influenced
by or manipulated by society and the people in my life.

I would say that I am (very loyal to myself / usually loyal to myself / more of a people pleaser
than I ought to be).

Being loyal to myself is sometimes hard because _____

but the greatest benefit is _____

Doing this dare taught me _____

_____

CONGRATULATIONS ON YOUR SUCCESS

ACCOMPLISHED
Loyalty Dare 5

After reading this dare, I can honestly say that I believe I am better at (having a friend / being a friend / neither / both) because _____

_____

Which statement from the "Explore What Kind of Friend You Are" is the most difficult for you to do and why? _____

_____

'The kind of friend I aim to be' and 'the kind of friend I am right now' are:

(Very Different / Somewhat Different / Somewhat Alike / Very Alike)

To be a better friend to my friends, I would like to work on or practice being

more _____ and less _____

Did you share your paper with a least 1 friend? Yes / No

If Yes, who was it and how did it go? If No, why not? _____

_____

The most important piece of information I want to remember from this dare is

_____

_____

If being a friend means bringing out the best in your friend and always wanting the best for them, then I would have to say that the person who is the best friend to me would be

_____ and the person I am the best friend to would be

_____ .

CONGRATULATIONS ON YOUR SUCCESS

ACCOMPLISHED
Loyalty Dare 6

I accomplished this dare by doing my best with _____

and _____ for 3 consecutive days.

I found it (extremely hard / somewhat difficult / not too hard / very easy) to do my best

and it made me feel _____

What seems to motivate you to do your best most often? (competition? love? reward?

positive attitude? being watched by others?) _____

_____

When I am not doing my best, it is usually because I am not (clear about what my best would
be / confident I can do it / committed to doing my best).

Of all the people I know, _____ is the one I believe tries
their hardest to always do their best.

What does the above person do or have that causes you to believe that about them? (positive
attitude? greater skills? confidence? commitment? focus?)

_____

_____

What is 1 thing you can do that can motivate you to always do your best.

   1.) _____

What do you believe accomplishing this dare taught you and how will you continue to

use it? _____

_____

CONGRATULATIONS ON YOUR SUCCESS

CHAPTER REVIEW

What is your favorite quote from this chapter? Why?

_____

_____

Which of the dares was the hardest? Why?

_____ because _____

_____

_____

Which of the dares was the easiest? Why?

_____ because _____

_____

_____

Which dare made you feel the best about what you had done? Why?

_____ because _____

_____

_____

Which dare do you think you will try to do most often? Why?

_____ because _____

_____

_____

Which dare did you do the most? # _____

Which dare did you do the least? # _____

Which dare was easiest to remember? # _____ hardest? # _____

Which dare had the most shocking/dramatic results? # _____ why? _____

_____

Which dare or dares did people seem to notice when you did it? _____

What did you learn about yourself and/or others through this chapter's exercises?

_____

_____

_____

_____

_____

_____

_____

_____

Can you think of another way to dare yourself in order to test or build-up this virtue?

_____

_____

_____

_____

_____

_____

_____

_____

_____

What was fun about these exercises? _____

_____

_____

What was not so fun? _____

_____

Use these 2 pages to keep notes during the week, jot down ideas or thoughts, or to evaluate your success. Set goals to help you accomplish the dares and goals for practicing them in the future.

_____

_____

_____

_____

_____

_____

_____

_____

_____

_____

_____

_____

_____

_____

_____

_____

_____

_____

_____

_____

_____

_____

_____

_____

_____

_____

_____

"It is not because things are difficult that we do not dare; it is because we do not dare that things are difficult."

~Seneca

"Lack of loyalty is one of the major causes of failure
in every walk of life."

Napoleon Hill

CHAPTER 8

OPTIMISM/POSITIVITY

Optimism: inclination to hopefulness and confidence. (Positive thinking)

Pessimism: tendency to take the worst view; expect the worst outcome.(Negative thinking)

As defined by *The Oxford illustrated Dictionary*

The Choice

Virtue: Optimistic

or

Vice: Pessimistic

The greatest two benefits of being optimistic or having a positive attitude are:

1.) _____

2.) _____

The two most detrimental consequences of being pessimistic or negative are:

1.) _____

2.) _____

Optimism/Positivity Agreement

I, _____, understand that being optimistic and positive are more beneficial to me than being pessimistic and negative. Therefore, I agree to read the following chapter, answer the questions presented, complete any exercises, and attempt to accomplish as many dares as possible – as often as I can.

Signed: _____   Date: _____

Dare 1

"Once you replace negative thoughts with positive ones, you will start having positive results."

~Willie Nelson

Dare to replace negative words with positive ones.

It is estimated that the average person thinks about 40 to 50 thousand thoughts a day and will speak nearly 15,000 words. As you have probably learned already in science class, we are made up of energy and all living things need energy to survive. What you might not know is that our words also have energy and will send out either positive or negative vibrations as we speak them. Try to feel the energy in these two sentences: "I am sooo mad," or "I am so frustrated I can't even think straight." When you have thoughts like these or speak these words out loud, you send out a negative vibration, or burst of energy, that attracts events, people, and objects with the same negative vibration. In Science, this occurrence is often called The Law of Attraction - which simply means, energies that are alike are attracted to one another. In her book, *Personal Power through Awareness*, Sanaya Roman says it this way, "Your thoughts are magnetic; they go out from you and draw to you those things you think about." Unfortunately, many of our thoughts and words are filled with negative energy and create a negative vibration that attracts to us exactly what we **don't** want. However, we do have the power to shift negative energy into positive energy at any given moment - IF we choose to do so. Truth is, controlling what thoughts come into our head is far more difficult than controlling what words come out of our mouths. Therefore, it may be easier to start being more positive by practicing replacing your negative words with positive ones when negativity is ruining your day. Saying positive, high energy words like AMAZING, ABUNDANT, VIBRANT, SENSATIONAL or EXCEPTIONAL can raise your energy quickly. Also, using the two most powerful, creative words in the world – I AM, before words like inspired, motivated, encouraged and optimistic is also a great way to attract good things to you. Even though a positive perspective is always only a thought away and will be far more effective at attracting what you **do** want, limiting or eliminating words filled with negative energy, or which have a low vibrational frequency, is a great place to start creating positive changes in your life.

To accomplish this dare: For 3 days, try to replace any negative words with positive ones. Get a blank index card and write the letters A-L on the front (2 columns of 6) and M-Z on the back. Next to each letter, write 3 of the most positive words, that begin with that letter, you can think of. Try to pick words that are descriptive adjectives like – Amazing, Powerful, Unique, and Valuable. Keep the index card with you and use it to help you shift your energy. For example: If you say, "That pop quiz made me so angry," the negative word and/or feeling here is – angry. Because angry starts with an 'a,' you will use one of the 'a' words on your index card to replace the negative energy with positive energy. Use the 'a' word from your card to complete this sentence 3 times – "I AM _____!" Complete the exercise on the following page to help you practice.

In each of the following sentences, circle the word with the lowest or most negative energy. These are often words that will be emphasized or stressed when spoken. Other times, they will follow an emphasized or stressed word- like 'so.'

"I just caught Donna talking poorly about me in the gym. That makes me so mad!"

"Did you see Mike knock Jeff's books out of his arms? He is so mean sometimes."

"My math grade is dropping rapidly and I feel so overwhelmed because of the amount of homework we have to do just to keep up."

"I got grounded because I failed my chemistry test. My parents are so unfair."

"I love John with all my heart, but he can be such a jerk at times."

"I have to finish my history paper by Monday. This weekend is going to suck."

From the following list of words, circle any words that you think are positive or have a high energy vibration when spoken. Then, put a line through any words which you believe are negative or have a low energy vibration.

Happy	Thankful	Guilty	Loving	Anxious	Caring
Beautiful	Dull	Considerate	Dumb	Magnificent	Noble
Afraid	Jealous	Optimistic	Shameful	Weak	Loyal
Doubtful	Dedicated	Powerful	Worried	Humble	Joyful
Passionate	Fearful	Frustrated	Qualified	Problem	Inspired
Hopeful	Ugly	Mean	Regretful	Productive	Calm
Amazing	Pathetic	Useless	Awful	Awesome	Worthy
Vibrant	Sad	Lazy	Smart	Truthful	Hate
Believe	Trapped	Sincere	Generous	Greedy	Free
Aggravated	Proud	Confident	Critical	Excellent	Perfect

List 3 words that you love to say and which you believe can raise your energy quickly.

_____   _____   _____

List 3 words that you often say which may be better left out of your vocabulary because they seem to bring you down or drain your energy.

_____   _____   _____

Food for Thought: This dare is not trying to get you to ignore or hide your negative feelings. The goal of this dare is to help you see how beneficial it is to fill your day with as many positive and high energy words as possible. Just because you are **u**pset doesn't mean you can't also be **u**nderstanding or **u**nique. You may still be upset, but focusing on being understanding and unique can help lessen the amount of negative energy you have as well as the amount of negative vibrations you are sending out to others while you're upset.

Dare 2

"The greatest weapon against stress is our ability to choose one thought over another."
~William James

Dare to speak more positive things than negative.

If someone was hired to record everything you say within a day and then file your words away as either positive or negative, you might be surprised at the amount of days in which your negative words outweigh the positive. Have you ever considered how negative thinking affects your life and your relationships? Truth is, your thoughts have a direct and powerful effect on your reality. People who are constantly focusing their attention on the negative things in life or whose thinking is habitually negative are often said to have a negative attitude or a 'what's wrong' mentality. Unlike the 'what's right' mentality which causes us to appreciate what is going right, compliment what we like, and expect the best…the 'what's wrong' mentality keeps us complaining, criticizing, and expecting the worse. Although negative habitual thinking is very common, we are not hardwired to think that way. As William James claims in his quote above, we have the ability to choose between positive and negative thoughts. Yet, so many of us excel at the 'what's wrong with this picture' game and fail to see how playing this game negatively affects our reality. Positive thinking 100% of the time is extremely difficult, but speaking more positive thoughts than negative ones in any given day is a good way to develop a more positive attitude. Acknowledging our power to choose one thought over another will help us focus our attention on the positive things in life and ultimately create a more positive reality.

To accomplish this dare: For 3 days, speak more positive thoughts than negative by avoiding complaining, criticizing and being negative. This will require you to monitor your words. You might think that you always monitor what you say, but in actuality, much of what you speak has not been thoroughly processed in your mind before it comes out of your mouth. That is why you sometimes regret what you say, wish you could take back what you have said, or question why you said it in the first place. If you are struggling to accomplish this dare, it may be helpful to set a 2:1 ratio as your goal. Any time you catch yourself saying something negative, follow it up with 2 positive statements. If you do this, the positive things said at the end of the day will outweigh the negative 2 to 1. Throughout the day, look for 'what's right,' acknowledge the good things that happen, and try being very complimentary to others.

Be Aware: What you seek, you will find! Expecting something to go wrong, invites it. That is why it is so important to use your power to choose the thoughts that work for you! Shifting from a negative thought into a positive thought doesn't happen over time, it happens in a moment. However, training yourself to be in the habit of having your positive thoughts outweigh your negative thoughts everyday may take a little more time and effort.

Most of my negative thinking is focused on (circumstances / other people / myself)

When I say negative things about people, I think I do it because: (Circle any that are true)

  a.) I am angry at them
  b.) I am trying to persuade others to agree with me
  c.) I am trying to defend myself because they attacked me first
  d.) It makes me feel better about myself
  e.) I am trying to help them be a better person
  f.) Other _____

I do more (criticizing / complaining) on a daily basis.

I tend to complain about: (Check any that are true and make up 1 of your own)

  _____ things I have to do (chores, errands, projects)
  _____ school or having too much homework
  _____ the way others act or treat me (parents, friends, employers)
  _____ what other people have but I don't / what I believe I lack
  _____ things I can't control (weather, laws, taxes)
  _____

I am better at (finding the good / identifying the flaws) in people.

I would prefer for people to (find the good in me / find my flaws).

During difficult situations or challenging times, I tend to: (Check any that are true)

  _____ focus on what went wrong or what did I do wrong
  _____ question why this is happening to me
  _____ dwell on how unfair people are or how hard life is
  _____ deny it even happened or refuse to deal with it
  _____ consider my options and look for what I can learn from it or what good can
          come out of it

What are 2 benefits of being positive? _____

_____

_____

What are 2 consequences of being negative? _____

_____

_____

Food for Thought: This dare is designed to help you see what kind of thinking is dominating your thoughts and aims to redirect your focus away from complaining and criticizing and onto complimenting and appreciating what is good in your life. At times, being positive might seem impossible, but in truth…it's always just a thought away.

Dare 3

"Your net worth to the world is usually determined by what remains after your bad habits are subtracted from your good ones."
~Benjamin Franklin

Dare to replace a bad habit with a good habit.

In a famous quote attributed to a man named Frank Outlaw, we are warned to watch our actions because they become habits and watch our habits because they become our character. Some of our behaviors/actions create positive results and are beneficial for us while others create negative results and are detrimental to us. However, getting positive results does not guarantee that we will make the action a habit any more than getting negative results can guarantee that we will stop it! Ironically, developing healthy or beneficial habits are often hard to do; yet, developing bad habits are often too easy to do. For example, eating healthy, taking vitamins, and exercising regularly are typically considered good behaviors, but it can be very difficult to develop a steady habit of doing these things. Waiting until the last minute to study for your exams is clearly a bad decision, but it can be very easy to establish this kind of study habit. There is an old proverb that states, "Bad habits are like a comfortable bed, easy to get into but hard to get out of." The good news is that there is also a flip side to that Truth and it can be found in Robert Puller's quote, "Good habits, once established, are just as hard to break as are bad habits." Truth is, judging an action as either good or bad is not nearly as important as acknowledging the choice we have to either make it a habit or stop doing it (based on whether the action is beneficial or detrimental to us). Unfortunately, we often do the things that we shouldn't be doing or don't want to do and put off the things that we want to do and/or ought to be doing. As a result, our habits, which are a direct reflection of our choices, are frequently more detrimental to us than they are beneficial. Making different choices will produce different actions. Any good action can become a steady habit if you just take the time to practice doing it, and any bad habit can be broken if you choose to STOP IT! When it comes to breaking a bad habit, the decision to stop doing it **should** be enough - but rarely ever is. So, it may be helpful to replace the bad habit with a good habit. For example, if you want to quit eating chips between meals, you may decide to eat a healthier snack, like fruits or vegetables, instead. Practicing a good habit, while trying to eliminate a bad one, can help to keep you motivated and may even make the change a little less difficult.

To accomplish this dare: Complete the exercise on the following page and then choose one of the following 3 methods to accomplish this dare. 1.) Attempt to replace 3 bad habits with 3 good ones for at least 1 day each. This means you have to pick 3 bad habits you want to replace with the opposite good habit and practice each one for 1 day. 2.) Attempt to replace 1 bad habit with the opposite good action for a full 3 day period. 3.) Attempt to do method 1 first, and then follow it up with method 2. This would mean you will have to spend 6 days working on this dare but can possibly eliminate up to 3 bad habits; quite a challenge!

Below are 15 habits that are generally considered bad or often produce negative results. On the line before each action, record how often you do each. Use "A" for always, "O" for often, "S" for sometimes, "R" for rarely, and "N" for never. The good/healthy action below each is there in case you want to try replacing that habit with the opposite.

_____ Waiting until the last minute to do a project or study for a test.
        Study or work on a project a little each night.

_____ Assuming I know what other people are thinking.
        Asking others what they are thinking.

_____ Eating too much junk food and/or candy.
        Eating healthy snacks and treats.

_____ Staying up too late and not getting enough sleep.
        Going to bed early enough to get a healthy full night's rest.

_____ Talking poorly about others or criticizing people.
        Complimenting or encouraging others.

_____ Using bad (foul) or disrespectful language.
        Using respectful language like Ma'am, Sir, Please, and Thank You.

_____ Writing fast and messy.
        Taking your time to write neat.

_____ Spending too much money or taking it for granted.
        Saving money.

_____ Talking just to be talking and giving every little detail in a story.
        Valuing your words and getting your point across in very few words.

_____ Expecting the worst to happen and/or being negative.
        Expecting the best and/or being positive.

_____ Being nosey and/or invading other's privacy.
        Respecting other's privacy and/or not snooping into other's business.

_____ Being selfish or greedy.
        Being generous, considerate of others, and appreciative.

_____ Pushing my beliefs and/or opinions on others.
        Respecting other's right to their own opinions.

_____ Making up excuses or lies to get out of trouble or to get the approval of others.
        Telling the Truth and accepting the consequences.

_____ Interrupting others while they are talking or being rude by not listening.
        Letting others finish their sentences and listening when others are talking.

List 2 habits below that you want to break and 2 good habits you can replace them with.

1.) _____

_____

2.) _____

_____

Dare 4

"All men make mistakes, but only wise men learn from their mistakes."

~Winston Churchill

Dare to encourage yourself to learn from so-called 'mistakes'.

Every day, we make hundreds of choices. Some of our choices have results that we like; we call these 'good' choices. Other choices have results that we don't like; we call these 'bad' choices or 'mistakes'. When we make choices that do not benefit us or which result in a negative experience, we tend to focus first on 'what' the undesired consequences or negative results are of our choice. Then, we focus on 'how' to deal with or avoid the negative consequences as best we can. Although acknowledging what the consequences of our choices are and considering how to respond are important things to do, they often keep us from focusing on something more important – 'Why?' Truth is, the most important thing to do when you make a 'mistake' is to learn from it. In order to learn from a 'mistake', you need to focus on the choice itself and not solely on the consequences and best possible responses. Asking yourself "Why are things the way they are?" forces you to look back at what choice you made that led to the undesired results and take responsibility for your choice. Then, you can try to determine 'why' you made that choice and 'why' did it create such undesirable results. By inquiring into 'why' your choice didn't get the desired results, you expose the need to do something different or make a different choice. In other words, you learn what **not** to do! Thomas Edison put it this way, "I haven't failed, I've found 10,000 ways that don't work." Learning is about taking what you know and applying it to what you do – it is all about the change. The reason people make the same mistakes over and over again is because they have not yet learned to change their choice. Sometimes, dealing with the consequences and choosing our response will need to be done immediately. However, it is very important to take the time to reflect on 'why' we made the choice we did and identify what different and better choice could we make if the same thing happens again.

To accomplish this dare: Use the exercise on the following page to help you learn from 2 of your past mistakes. Then, identify a choice that you are currently making or have recently made which will likely have a negative result and learn from it. Remember, for learning to occur – change has to happen. So, you will need to find something you do regularly that creates undesirable results and actually do something different and better.

(Ex: Instead of waiting till the last minute to study, you could study a little each night.)

Be Aware: Negative experiences are not always evidence that we made a 'mistake' or 'bad' choice. Sometimes, things happen to us that are out of our control or are the result of someone else's choices. Even if you are not responsible for what happened, you can still choose how you will respond and whether you want to learn from the experience or not.

To practice learning from your mistakes, **D.A.R.E.** to follow these simple steps:

D – **D**etermine what your original goal or desired result was. (What did you want or lose?)

A – **A**cknowledge what action or choice kept you from achieving that goal or caused the undesirable or negative result. (What was your mistake? What did or didn't you do?)

R – **R**eflect on the reason for your choice or action and rationalize why you got the results that you did. (Why did I choose to do what I did and what results did I expect?)

E - **E**xplore what may be a better action or choice that will help you to achieve the goal or desired result. (What can I do differently or better if this happens again?)

Example: Your best friend since the 3rd grade just did something that really made you mad. You get revenge by exposing your friend's deepest and darkest secrets to anyone who is willing to listen. Your original goal was to be a good friend. Your mistake was betraying your friend's trust by exposing their secrets. Why you did it was because you were hurt and angry and you thought attacking back would make you feel better. A wiser choice may have been to remain a trustworthy and loyal friend even though you were hurt and mad.

Use 2 actions or choices from your past that had negative results to complete the following:

1.) What was the original goal or desired result? _____

State the choice or action that you now consider to be a mistake? What did/didn't you do?

_____

Why did you make that choice and why do you think you got those results? _____

_____

What might have been a better choice? _____

2.) What was the original goal or desired result? _____

State the choice or action that you now consider to be a mistake? What did/didn't you do?

_____

Why did you make that choice and why do you think you got those results? _____

_____

What might have been a better choice? _____

_____

List 2 things that you do that often produce negative results and you really want to change.

1. _____   2. _____

Dare 5

"We have to learn to be our own best friend because we fall too easily into the trap of being your own worst enemy."   ~Roderick Thorp-Rainbow Drive

Dare to silence your inner critic and judge.

What would you do if someone was saying something negative, mean, disrespectful, or discouraging to your best friend? If you are a good friend, you probably wouldn't stand for it. You may correct the person with evidence of the opposite, counter-attack by calling the person out on their poor behavior, or simply ignore them and walk away. It's natural for people to want to protect or defend their friends when they are being verbally and emotionally mistreated or abused. It's also natural for people to try to defend or protect themselves when they feel attacked or threatened by others. In psychology, these two natural reactions are called the 'Fight' or 'Flight' responses. For most people, being verbally, emotionally, or physically abused or mistreated is considered unacceptable and will result in one of these two natural responses. However, when it comes to that little, or in most cases – BIG, voice in our head that loves to bully us, our typical response is rarely a natural one. Truth is, our own criticisms, negativity, and judgments often make us our own worst enemies. Refusing to fight, or take flight from, your 'inner critic' and 'judge' is like inviting an enemy to follow you around all day and encouraging them to tell you everything they don't like about you, point out everything you do wrong, remind you of every mistake you have ever made, and persuade you to believe that you are not (nor will you ever be) worthy or deserving of anything good. Can you imagine what kind of impact this would have on your energy levels, self esteem, and sense of self worth by the end of day? So, if you wouldn't want your enemies following you around for even a day, it is a good idea not to invite or allow one to live in your head for the rest of your life.

To accomplish this dare: For 3 days within a week's time frame, silence your inner critic and judge by using one or both of the following methods. Method One: Take a day of vacation from your inner critic and judge. Whenever your inner critic and judge attempts to reach you, send them straight to voicemail. Create an automatic message to be used throughout the day that sounds something like this: "I am not available today because I am on vacation. Feel free to try back on Wednesday." Whatever you do, do not add a beep for your inner critic and judge to leave a message because IT will. Method Two: Always have a positive "Maybe, BUT" response to anything negative, disrespectful, discouraging, or mean your inner critic and judge says to you. For example, if your inner judge says "You really messed things up this time," you can reply "Maybe, BUT there's still a chance I can get it right next time." By using the word 'maybe', you avoid confirming whether or not what your inner critic and judge said is true. The whole point of the exercise is to avoid beating yourself up, regardless if it's true, by finding a positive perspective to focus on.

My inner critic (is always talking / talks a lot / sometimes talks / rarely talks / never talks).

List 2 things your inner critic would say is wrong with your body. _____

_____

List 2 things your inner critic would say is bad about your character/personality? _____

_____

What 2 mistakes does your inner judge like to remind you of? _____

_____

Finish the following 3 sentences from your inner judge's perspective.

    You do not deserve to _____

    You are not worthy of _____

    You are incapable of _____

Your inner critic diminishes your self esteem by putting you down, pointing out your flaws, and attempting to make you believe that others are better than you. Your inner judge diminishes your sense of self worth by trying to make you feel guilty for your mistakes, telling you that you are incapable of what you are trying or wanting to do, and trying to convince you that you are not worthy or deserving of anything good.

Which one do you think talks to you the most and how does that voice make you feel?

_____

_____

Which one is harder to live with and why? _____

_____

Food for Thought: You may think the goal of this dare is to help you to get rid of your inner critic and judge forever. However, this is NOT the case. Our inner critic and judge do serve a purpose and can be very beneficial to our personal growth. By defending yourself to your inner critic and protecting yourself from your inner judge, you let them know that you refuse to be bullied by them any longer. At first, they may attack you more than usual. However, the more you practice this dare, the faster they will learn that you aren't going to listen to them unless they are being respectful, honest, positive, and/or helpful. The main goal of the dare is to help you to protect your self esteem and self worth by learning how to silence your inner critic and judge. The ultimate goal would be to convince your inner critic and judge to become your own best friend. Because, making your inner critic and judge into a friend, actually eliminates your own worst enemy.

Dare 6

"When you are immune to the opinions and actions of others, you won't be the victim of needless suffering."
~Don Miguel Ruiz

"Whenever someone is pushing your buttons, remember... You are the one who installed them!"
~C. Leslie Charles

Dare to stop taking the opinions or actions of others personally.

When others say negative things about us or do something we're offended or hurt by, we will either take it personally or we won't. If we take it personally, we almost instantly become defensive, feel sad, or even get angry, but if we don't take it personally, the negative opinions and/or hurtful actions of others will have little or no effect on us at all. In his book, *The Four Agreements*, Don Miguel Ruiz teaches that what others do, say, and think is all about them - not about you. He asserts that, "Nothing other people do (or say) is because of you; it IS because of themselves," and for that reason - we should not take anything personally. However, not taking the negative opinions or hurtful actions of others personally is often very difficult to do. Why? According to Don Miguel, "What someone says will only affect you if you believe it." Truth is, whether or not we take the negative opinions and/or hurtful actions of others personally, or not, depends more on what we think of ourselves than on what others think of us. In his book, *Learned Optimism*, psychologist Martin E. P. Seligman describes **Personalization** as a person's habitual way of explaining bad events as either caused by Internal or External factors. He states, ""Because of Me" thoughts represent self-blame (internality)." For example: If John didn't invite me to his party, it must be because I'm a geek. ""Because of Someone or Something Else" thoughts represent externality." For example: If John didn't invite me to his party, it's probably because he is friends with my ex-boyfriend and John didn't want him to feel uncomfortable at the party. An optimistic person with high self-esteem rarely takes anything others say or do personally; whereas a pessimistic person with low self-esteem usually takes everything others say or do personally. Therefore, if you really want to avoid being negatively affected by what others do or say, what you think and how you feel about yourself needs to become far more important to you than what others may think or feel about you.

To accomplish this dare: Complete the exercises on the following page; the second one is a version of Dr. Seligman's Exercise in *The Optimistic Child*. On 3 occasions when you feel angry, hurt, insulted, or criticized by something someone says or does, find an optimistic response that will help you to avoid taking things personally.

Be Aware: Don Miguel Ruiz describes anger, jealousy, criticisms, insults, sadness, and fear as forms of 'emotional poison.' When it comes to what others say or do, accepting that '**everything is not all about you**', and developing the attitude of '**what others think about me is really none of my business**', can make you immune to their emotional poison.

For each of the following events, put an "O" in front of the following sentence that represents an optimistic perspective and a "P" in front of the sentence that is pessimistic.

Our team lost bad Friday night. _____ Our team just doesn't have any talent.
_____ The other team played a better game than we did.

I ran for class president but lost. _____ My opponent did a great job campaigning for votes
_____ I am not as popular as I thought I was.

My mom and I fight all the time. _____ I always make my mom mad no matter what I do.
_____ My mom and I just have conflicting personalities.

I failed my math exam. _____ I am not smart enough to pass that class
_____ I didn't prepare as well as I should have.

Jenny just called me stupid. _____ Jenny disagrees with my decision to forgive Sam.
_____ I probably am stupid for forgiving Sam.

Bill keeps talking over me. _____ I must not be an interesting person
_____ Bill is better at talking than he is at listening.

I won the raffle at school. _____ I guess even I can get lucky every now and then.
_____ I deserved to win; I bought a bunch of tickets!

"Because of me," or "What else can it be?" Exercise

For each of the following events, identify what the "Because of me" thought would be, describe how that thought would make you feel, and consider what reaction you might have. Then, you will do the same steps for the "What else can it be" thought.

Example Event: You invite your friend to come over after school and hang out but they decide to go to another friend's house instead.

"Because of Me" thought: *"I must not be as fun as his/her other friend is or maybe I did something that made my friend mad."*

What feelings and reactions might you have? *This thought makes me feel sad and my reaction is to cry or I feel angry and rejected so I'm going to ignore my friend for a few days to get even.*

"What else could it be" thought: *"I know that my friend and his/her friend are in the same class and have a big test tomorrow. They are probably getting together to study."*

What feelings and reactions might you have? *This thought makes me feel happy for my friend and I will just make plans to get together with my friend tomorrow instead.*

Do each of the 4 events either in your mind or on a piece of loose leaf.

Event 1 – You come home from school and go to the kitchen to get a snack. Your mom is in the kitchen cooking dinner and starts yelling at you for eating a handful of chips. She calls you inconsiderate and tells you how unappreciated and disrespected she feels because you ate a snack even though you saw her cooking dinner.

Event 2 - Your boyfriend/girlfriend breaks up with you and doesn't give you a reason why.

Event 3 - You're sick for a week but none of your friends come by to see how you are.

Event 4 – Your parents won't let you sleep at a friend's house if their parents aren't there.

ACCOMPLISHED
Optimism/Positivity Dare 1

Accomplishing this dare was (extremely difficult / harder than I thought it would be / not too difficult / fairly easy).

How did you feel when you were making your index card of positive, high energy words?

_____

I was (shocked / pleased / disappointed / _____) by the amount of negative or low energy words I said throughout the 3 day period.

What effect or impact did this exercise have on your attitude or experiences during those

3 days? _____

_____

What did you learn from doing this dare or what do you really want to remember about it?

_____

_____

I believe that the greatest benefit of continuing to practice this dare would be _____

_____

_____

In Sanaya Roman's book, she suggests to create positive words from the letters you see on a car's license plate. (Of course, you know that you shouldn't be the one driving while playing that game!) What is another way you could practice this dare without having to carry around an index card?

_____

_____

CONGRATULATIONS ON YOUR SUCCESS

Optimism/Positivity Dare 2

Being more positive than negative for 3 consecutive days took

(no effort / a little effort / more effort than I thought / a lot of effort)

I accomplished this dare

    a.) on the first try; without ever having to ever start over

    b.) on my second attempt; when I was more determined and focused

    c.) after numerous attempts because a negative day kept getting in the way

Which day was the hardest to get through? (1st day / 2nd day / 3rd day) Why?

_____

I monitored my words (a lot more / a little bit more / about the same as).

What are a few things you learned about yourself through doing this dare? _____

_____

_____

How did you feel at the end of the third consecutive day of being positive? _____

_____

Did you use the 2:1 ratio to help you accomplish the dare? Yes / No If Yes, how effective

were you at applying it and did it help? _____

_____

Redirecting my thinking away from 'what's wrong' by focusing on 'what's right' was (very easy / somewhat easy / somewhat difficult / difficult) and I believe it was (almost always / only sometimes / rarely ever / never) helpful.

Will you continue to practice being more positive than negative? Yes / No

CONGRATULATIONS ON YOUR SUCCESS

ACCOMPLISHED
Optimism/Positivity Dare 3

I accomplished this dare by:

    a.) Replacing 3 bad habits with 3 good habits for 1 day each,

    b.) Replaced 1 bad habit for 1 good habit for a 3 day period,

    c.) Both A and B

What were the 3 habits you listed that you wanted to break?

    1.) _____

    2.) _____

    3.) _____

Were you able to stop doing these actions for at least 1 day each? Yes / No

If Yes, Congrats and Keep practicing doing this until your bad habit is gone.

If No, why not? _____

★★★Note: Your level of success will depend on your level of commitment.★★★

What would be the benefit of breaking each of the above bad habits?

Habit 1: _____

Habit 2: _____

Habit 3: _____

Which habit would be the hardest to break? 1 – 2 – 3   Easiest? 1 – 2 – 3

Do you believe that you can break all 3 of these habits? Yes / No

★★★Note: Remember the quote by Henry Ford, "Whether you think you can or think you can't – you are right." So, think you can – and you will.

The most important thing I learned from doing this dare was _____

_____

CONGRATULATIONS ON YOUR SUCCESS

Optimism/Positivity Dare 4

Doing the D.A.R.E exercise on the 2 mistakes from my past was (very easy / easy / not so easy / difficult)

If either of these 2 situations occurred again, would you make the same choice or mistake?

Yes / No If No, what will you do instead? _____

_____

What current or recent mistake did you choose to learn from? _____

_____

What did you do different and was this choice better? _____

_____

Rank the statements below according to how difficult or easy they will be for you. Use '1' to identify what will be easiest to do and '8' to identify the most difficult.

_____ State what the original goal or desired result was.

_____ Assume responsibility for the mistake; hold myself accountable.

_____ Identify the choice/choices which lead to the undesired results.

_____ Determine why I made that choice and why were the results negative.

_____ Avoid repeating mistake; learn what NOT to do.

_____ Create a better choice or plan of action for achieving the goal.

_____ Develop a habit of seeking what my experiences can teach me.

_____ Appreciate 'mistakes' by seeing them as opportunities to grow.

If done on a regular basis, what benefits could this dare produce? _____

_____

This dare taught me _____

CONGRATULATIONS ON YOUR SUCCESS

Optimism/Positivity Dare 5

Accomplishing this dare was (very difficult / somewhat difficult / not too difficult / fairly easy)

I used (method 1 / method 2) most often.

Which method was more fun? 1 or 2 Which method worked better? 1 or 2

What did this dare teach you about your inner critic and judge? _____

_____

What are 3 things that your inner critic or judge says about you that you will no longer

listen to? _____

_____

_____

What would be the greatest benefit of having your inner critic and judge as a friend

instead of an enemy? _____

_____

To be a better friend to myself, I need to: (Circle as many as you want) (compliment myself more often / forgive myself if I make a mistake / be more understanding and compassionate with myself / be more loyal to myself / stop comparing myself to others / celebrate my good qualities and accomplishments / respect myself more / be less critical of myself / be more loving and accepting of myself / stand up for myself / find myself worthy)

The most important piece of information I want to remember from this dare is _____

_____

TRUTH AND DARE

CONGRATULATIONS ON YOUR SUCCESS

ACCOMPLISHED
Optimism/Positivity Dare 6

I found it (extremely hard / somewhat difficult / not too hard / very easy) to stop taking the negative opinions or hurtful actions of others personally.

I learned that I am (always / often / sometimes / rarely / never) optimistic and I am (always / often / sometimes / rarely / never) pessimistic.

Describe 1 of the 3 occasions when you applied the "Because of me," or "What else can it be" exercise to avoid taking something someone said or did personally.

What was the negative opinion or hurtful action that caused you to feel angry, hurt,

insulted, disrespected, or criticized? _____

_____

What results did you get when you applied the steps from the exercise to this event?

_____

_____

The exercise was (very / somewhat / not at all) effective at helping me to avoid taking what was said or done personally.

What do you believe accomplishing this dare taught you _____

_____

What are 2 benefits of not taking the negative opinions or hurtful actions of others personally?

   1.) _____

   2.) _____

CONGRATULATIONS ON YOUR SUCCESS

CHAPTER REVIEW

What is your favorite quote from this chapter? Why?

_____

_____

Which of the dares was the hardest? Why?

_____ because _____

_____

_____

Which of the dares was the easiest? Why?

_____ because _____

_____

_____

Which dare made you feel the best about what you had done? Why?

_____ because _____

_____

_____

Which dare do you think you will try to do most often? Why?

_____ because _____

_____

_____

Which dare did you do the most? # _____

Which dare did you do the least? # _____

Which dare was easiest to remember? # _____ hardest? # _____

Which dare had the most shocking/dramatic results? # _____ why? _____

_____

Which dare or dares did people seem to notice when you did it? _____

What did you learn about yourself and/or others through this chapter's exercises?

_____

_____

_____

_____

_____

_____

_____

_____

Can you think of another way to dare yourself in order to test or build-up this virtue?

_____

_____

_____

_____

_____

_____

_____

_____

_____

_____

What was fun about these exercises? _____

_____

_____

What was not so fun? _____

_____

Use these 2 pages to keep notes during the week, jot down ideas or thoughts, or to evaluate your success. Set goals to help you accomplish the dares and goals for practicing them in the future.

_____

_____

_____

_____

_____

_____

_____

_____

_____

_____

_____

_____

_____

_____

_____

_____

_____

_____

_____

_____

_____

_____

_____

"It is not because things are difficult that we do not dare; it is because we do not dare that things are difficult."

~Seneca

"A pessimist sees the difficulty in every opportunity; an optimist sees the opportunity in every difficulty."

Winston Churchill

CHAPTER 9

AUTHENTICITY/SELF LOVE

Authentic: genuine (without disguise; an original).

Fake: not genuine; counterfeit (disguised; phony; imitation).

As defined by *The Oxford illustrated Dictionary*

The Choice

Virtue: Authentic

or

Vice: Fake

The greatest two benefits of being authentic are:

1.) _____

2.) _____

The two most detrimental consequences of being fake or phony are:

1.) _____

2.) _____

Authenticity/Self Love Agreement

I, _____, understand that being authentic is more beneficial to me than being fake. Therefore, I agree to read the following chapter, answer the questions presented, complete any exercises, and attempt to accomplish as many dares as possible - as often as I can.

Signed: _____   Date: _____

Dare 1

"Actions speak louder than words — but not as often."
~Mark Twain

"It is far more impressive when others discover your good qualities without your help."
~Unknown

Dare to let your actions represent you instead of your words.

Wouldn't it be great if people judged us on our good intentions instead of our actions? If they did, we would likely do a lot less boasting, bragging, and exaggerating about who we are. We wouldn't have to defend our reputation, convince people to accept us, prove how good we are, or use manipulation and force to make people like us. Having good intentions would be the only thing that mattered. In reality, however, good intentions are rarely ever enough. Our actions are what matter most and all the boasting, bragging, exaggerating, defending, manipulating, and arguing usually fail to be convincing. Sadly, not only are others unconvinced when we do these things, but often they become even less impressed! Blaise Pascal stated that, "If you wish for people to think well of you… don't speak well of yourself." Truth is, the best way to get others to think highly of you is to think highly enough about yourself to let your actions represent you. It will take courage and a lot of discipline to allow others to form and have their own opinions of you based solely on your behavior. As you continue to practice letting your actions represent you, your fear of rejection and your need for other's approval will slowly start to fade away. When this happens, you are more accepting of yourself and both your intentions and your actions become more authentic; now that would be impressive! Then, you might just learn that… The 'you' that you're trying to sell to others… pales in comparison to the Who You Really Are.

To accomplish this dare: For 3 days, allow others the right to form and have their own opinion of you. Avoid boasting about how great you are, bragging about something you have done, exaggerating to make yourself look better, defending your reputation, trying to sell yourself like a product, seeking the approval or acceptance of others, or using manipulation or persuasion to get others to change their mind about you or anyone else. Try to find as many opportunities as possible to say, "You have the right to your opinion and I do not feel the need to try and change it."

Be Aware: No matter how good your intentions and actions are, there will still be people who don't like you. Some may say negative things about you and others may do mean things just to hurt you. One of the greatest philosophers that ever existed gave the best advice about what to do when this happens. Plato taught, "When men speak ill of you…Live as though nobody will believe them." So, let them say what they want to say… no one is likely to believe them anyway.

Use N-for never, R-for rarely, S-for sometimes, O-for often, or A-for always to make each sentence true for you.

I _____ boast or talk about myself to others.   I _____ brag about the good things I do.

I _____ exaggerate the truth when I talk about myself or my accomplishments to others.

I _____ defend my reputation when others are talking negatively about me or are lying.

I _____ try to sell myself like a product by trying to get others to think they need me or that they are better off with me than they would be without me.

I _____ try to persuade others to change their minds about me if they don't like me.

I _____ try to convince others to have the same opinions as I do about other people.

I am _____ willing to let others form and have their own opinions about me and others.

My intentions are _____ better than my actions.

What do you think will be the hardest thing to avoid doing and why? _____

_____

Of all the people you know, who do you think would struggle the most trying to do this dare?

_____ Why? _____

_____

How do you feel when you are around this person, or what thoughts do you have when they do what you explained above? _____

_____

Who does a great job of letting their actions represent them? _____

Food for Thought: You are more likely to feel a need to justify or defend yourself to others when you know your actions are not as good as your intentions. For example, if your intention is to be an honest person but you often get caught in a lie, you will likely make excuses for or try to justify the lies to others. However, if you rarely ever lie and someone begins to publicly accuse you of being a liar, you will probably feel there is no need to defend yourself because you know that people are highly unlikely to believe them.

Dare 2

"If you must love your neighbor as yourself, it is at least fair to love yourself as your neighbor."
~Nicholas de Chamfort

"You YourSelf, as much as anybody in the entire universe, deserves your love and affection."
~Buddha

Dare to be as kind and loving with yourself as you are to the people you love.

Have you ever met someone who is really hard on themselves or who is excellent at mentally beating themselves up? To some degree, everyone is hard on themselves at some point or about certain things. Some people are really hard on themselves physically. They beat themselves up by trying to do too much or by forcing their body to look a certain way. Others push themselves mentally by setting extraordinary standards or expectations on themselves and often won't settle for anything less than perfection. Then, there are those who are hard on themselves emotionally. They are often 'people-pleasers' who will push themselves into doing anything just to be liked or accepted by others. Truth is, there is nothing wrong with pushing ourselves towards our goals, striving for perfection, or even trying to please others – except when we neglect to be kind and loving to ourselves in the process. Unfortunately, we often treat others better than we do ourselves. If a friend makes a mistake or hurts us, we may say… "It's OK – we all make mistakes" and quickly forgive them and move on. Yet, we beat ourselves up over nothing, refuse to forgive ourselves for everything, and won't leave the past behind us for anything. We encourage others to 'dream big' but tell ourselves to 'quit dreaming.' We extend compassion to others when they are hurting, but criticize, blame, or kick ourselves when we are down. We try to support the needs of others but often neglect our own. The good news is, we are just as capable of being kind, loving, forgiving, supportive, compassionate, and encouraging to ourselves as we are to others. The only thing we need to learn is that we are just as deserving of our love and kindness as they are. Then, all we have to do is be willing to extend to ourselves the same love and kindness that we give to others. By doing this, we learn to love ourselves more… and are able to love others even better!

To accomplish this dare: Use the following page to discover how, where, and when you are being unkind or unloving to yourself. Pick 2 things from the "What's good for You… is good for Me Exercise" and commit to doing each of them for at least 3 days. Also, determine which 2 actions or thoughts causes you the most stress or creates the biggest problems for you on a regular basis. For 3 days, commit to doing the opposite action or having the opposing positive thought for the 2 most harmful or detrimental actions or thoughts.

"What is good for You...is good for Me Exercise"

Think of a time when you have done each of the following: forgiven someone, advised someone to be compassionate with themselves, motivated someone to do something kind for themselves, supported someone's goal or dream, stood up for someone or encouraged someone to be more accepting of and loving to themselves. Then, complete the sentences.

Because I am willing and able to forgive others, I deserve to forgive myself for _____

_____

Because I am willing and able to advise others to be compassionate with themselves, I deserve

to be more compassionate with myself by _____

Because I am willing and able to motivate others to do something kind for themselves, I

deserve to treat myself to _____

Because I am willing and able to be supportive of other's goals/dreams, I deserve to be

more supportive of my goal/dream to _____

Because I am willing and able to stand up for others, I deserve to stand up for myself by

_____

Because I am willing and able to encourage others to accept and love themselves, I deserve

to be more loving and accepting of myself by _____

On the line before each action, indicate how often you do it by using N-for Never / R-for Rarely / S-for Sometimes / O-for Often / or A-for Always. Then, match each negative action/thought with the opposite or opposing positive action/thought in the other column.

Ex: I _A_ dwell on my mistakes------focus on what I do right or what I have accomplished

I _____ talk or think poorly about myself	I appreciate the things I have
I _____ expect the worst to happen	I am worthy of good things
I _____ criticize the way I look	I find the good in people/things
I _____ compare myself to others	I look for solutions to problems
I _____ doubt my skills or abilities	I Live in the Now, not the past
I _____ want for more than what I have	I compliment the way I look
I _____ judge myself as unworthy of anything good	I expect things to work out well
I _____ dwell on things from the past	I have faith in what I can do
I _____ complain about my problems	I speak/think well about myself
I _____ find what's wrong in everything/everyone	I don't compare myself to others

Dare 3

"**There is nothing noble about being superior to some other man. True nobility is in being superior to your previous self.**"

~ Hindu Proverb

Dare to avoid comparing yourself to others in order to determine your own value or worth.

The word 'compare' is often defined as an examination of the similarities and/or differences between two or more things. However, this definition does not expose the most common and harmful aspect of comparing – judgment. Unfortunately, we rarely make comparisons about anything without also making a judgment from the results. If you are comparing your hand me down jeans and dirty old tee-shirt to someone else's new American Eagle outfit, you are not likely looking to see if your shirts are the same color or if your jeans have the same amount of pockets – are you? Most often, when we compare what we have, how we look, and what we can do, to that of another, what we are actually doing is judging ourselves based on how we rank or compare to others. It's almost like we're imputing little 'greater than' or 'less than' signs into equations that look a bit like this: My appearance is (<) their appearance, My truck (<) her mustang, My grades are (<) my friend's grades. As you can imagine, it will be very difficult to maintain a high level of self esteem or a solid sense of self worth if you are frequently comparing yourself to others who end up winning the competition. Funny thing is… that's what we most often do! As a result, people often suffer from feelings of "I am not good enough," "I am not smart enough," "I am not pretty enough," and "I am not worthy enough." Truth is, how you look, what you have, and how your abilities or skills compare to others, does NOT determine your worth. In fact, what makes each of us so valuable is that we are unique and different from one another. Just like every snowflake has its own unique design, one no less beautiful than another, no two people are meant to be alike nor should their worth or value be judged by comparisons with that of another. The only person that can fairly be compared to 'who you currently are' is 'who you are capable of Being.' Even comparing yourself to who you once were is not a fair fight.

To accomplish this dare: Answer the questions on the following page and complete the "It's not FAIR to Compare," exercise. Then, use the FAIR acronym from the exercise on 3 more occasions when you begin to judge yourself as 'greater than' or 'less than,' based on how you rank or compare to someone else.

Be Aware: Comparing yourself to others is silly when you come to understand the Truth – You are actually always in the middle. Like the African Proverb states, "Whatever accomplishment you boast of, there is someone who can do it better than you." Just as there will always be someone who has less than you have, there will also be others who will most definitely have more.

TRUTH AND DARE

I (always / often / sometimes / rarely /never) compare my appearance to other people.

I (always / often / sometimes / rarely /never) compare what I have to what others have.

I (always / often / sometimes / rarely /never) compare my skills or talents to others.

When I compare myself to others, I often judge myself as (< / = / >) the other person.

What feelings or thoughts do you usually have when comparing yourself to someone else?

_____

_____

It's Not FAIR to COMPARE Exercise

- **F**ind 2 reasons why this comparison may not be fair
- **A**cknowledge and Appreciate
  - Acknowledge that you do not need to look like others, have what others have, or share the same skills and talents of others to be valuable.
  - Appreciate what you do have by considering how things could be worse.
- **I**dentify your Greatest Potential by considering what *your best would be* based on your current conditions. (Focus on what you can do, how you can look, and what's the best you can have.)
- **R**emember your worth and value come from Being the Best You can Be without regard to anyone else.

For each of the 3 situations below, apply the FAIR acronym to practice avoiding using comparisons to determine your worth or value.

Example situation: All my friends have smart phones and I don't.

F: This is not a fair comparison because I had a smart phone and broke it, so my parents won't let me get another one until it's time for an upgrade. Plus, my friends all have jobs and pay for their own phones, but I don't.

A: I acknowledge I don't need a smart phone even though I want one, and I really should appreciate the phone I have because many people don't even have that.

I: My greatest potential would be to practice being more respectful with my phone and wait patiently until I can get a new one.

R: I know that not having a new smart phone does not make me less valuable and is not as important as learning to be a respectful, patient, and grateful person.

1.) You and your best friend both tried out for a team sport. They made the team, but you didn't.

2.) Your best friend's parents just bought them a brand new car for their 16th birthday, and you got a hand me down used car from an older sibling as a graduation present.

3.) Your friend is 3 inches taller than you and is in much better shape than you are.

Dare 4

"**Wise men speak because they have something to say; fools because they have to say something.**"

~Plato

Dare to speak only what is worthy of being spoken.

There's an old Spanish Proverb that says, "Don't speak unless you can improve on silence." This would be a lot easier to do if we all had some kind of filter on our lips that would examine our thoughts before we spoke them. To get through this 'worthy of being spoken' filter, our words would have to be respectful, positive, valuable, useful, true, and considerate of other's feelings. Can you imagine how quiet and different the world would be if everyone had a filter like this? Truth is, if we want people to listen to us and value what we say, what we say should be valuable and worth listening to! Unfortunately, deciding whether or not something is worthy of being spoken can be a very difficult thing to do. Groucho Marx once said, "Before I speak, I **have** something important to say." For the purpose of this dare, you will use each of the letters in the word 'have' to help you determine what will make it through the 'worthy of being spoken' filter. The 'H' stands for honest; "Is what I want to say true?" The 'A' stands for admirable; "Is it respectable, harmless, and considerate of other's feelings?" The 'V' stands for valuable; "Is it useful, important, and relevant to the conversation?" The 'E' stands for encouraging; "Is it positive and inspiring?" If you can answer 'Yes' to at least 3 of these questions, then you actually _have_ something to say and should say it. If the answer is 'No' to more than 1 of these questions, then you _do not have_ anything to say and should remain silent. People who speak a little but say a lot are far more likely to keep the attention of others, than people who speak a lot but say a little. So, it benefits us to 'choose our words wisely.'

To accomplish this dare: For 2 consecutive days, speak only what is worthy of being spoken. An effective exercise that will help you to accomplish this dare can be found in William Penn's quote, "If thou thinkest twice before you speak, thou will speak twice the better for it." To think twice about something before saying it, take 5 seconds to ask yourself, "Is what I am about to say **h**onest, **a**dmirable, **v**aluable, or **e**ncouraging?" You do not need to do this if you are simply greeting someone or responding to a question. Try to imagine you're playing 'the quiet game' all day and the only way to stay in the game is to speak only the thoughts that would make it through the 'worthy of being spoken' filter.

Be Aware: You are likely going to realize very quickly that this dare is way harder than you thought it would be. Surveying your words and speaking only what is worthy of being said may result in you only speaking a few sentences throughout the day! The people around you will definitely notice. They may even think something is wrong, ask if you are mad at them, or wonder if you are feeling sick.

Fill in the blanks with 1 of the following: **Always, Often, Sometimes, Rarely, or Never**

1.) I _____ talk just to be talking.

2.) I _____ regret the things I say.

3.) I _____ really think about what I am going to say before I speak.

4.) I _____ use plenty of details and take a long time to get to the point.

5.) After I say something, I _____ reflect on what I said or question whether or not I should have said it.

6.) The things I say are _____ valuable, useful, or important.

7.) The things I say are _____ things everyone can hear.

8.) The things I say are _____ respectful, honorable and considerate of others.

9.) The things I say are _____ true / honest.

For me, the most difficult part of doing this dare may be _____

_____

Who do you think would struggle the most if they had to do this dare? _____

Why? _____

Who do you think would not have too much trouble at all doing this dare? _____

Why? _____

How could practicing to speak only what is worthy of being spoken benefit you? _____

_____

_____

Food for Thought: Consider the 2 people you listed above. Does one make for better company than the other? Does one seem to get better responses or reactions from the people they are talking to? Does one seem to have more drama and conflict in their life than the other? Who do you think regrets what they say more often? The best way to keep our feet out of our mouths is to remember: What we say, how we say it, why we say it, when we say it, and to whom we say it to… can only be regretted – **IF** we say it!

Dare 5

"Be who you are and say what you feel because those who mind don't matter and those who matter don't mind."

~Dr. Seuss

Dare to value 'You' more than the 'you' others want you to be.

Who is more important in a movie, the main character or an extra that is walking down the street as the main character's car speeds by? Which will always be worth more, an original Michelangelo picture or a fake copy of one? You probably didn't have to think very hard to answer either of those two questions; the answers were obvious. Here's one that might be a little more difficult. Who has the lead role in your movie and/or is most important in your Life, You or the you that others want you to be? Unfortunately, in an attempt to avoid conflict and gain the acceptance or approval of others, people often become experts at pretending to 'be someone they're not.' In his book, *Be Yourself, everyone else is already taken*, Mike Robbins describes this behavior as a 'disease to please.' He states, "Constantly trying to do or say the 'right' thing so others will approve of us, like us, and keep us in good favor does not empower us to be ourselves, speak our truth, or live our deepest passions." In other words, having a 'disease to please' is like playing an extra in someone else's life instead of Being the leading role in your own. Truth is, your authentic Self is far more important and valuable than anyone that you may pretend to be. You ARE an original, and to die a copy is a waste of '**Your Life**.' When it comes to the lead role in your life, there's no one more qualified and deserving for the part than You! In showbiz, the people who win the Oscars or Emmys are those who are the best at acting; in Life, the people who have the greatest rewards are those who don't need to act at all.

To accomplish this dare: Complete the exercise on the following page. Then, for 3 days, try to keep track of when you may be: people pleasing, sacrificing, being fake, conforming to the crowd, or being agreeable just to gain the approval of others or to avoid conflict. Also, notice and record times when you avoid these 5 actions and let your Authentic Self direct your behavior. The best way to keep track of your actions would be to carry around a sticky note and record them as they happen. If this is too difficult, record as many as you can remember on paper as soon after the event as possible or at the end of each day.

Be Aware: Being your Authentic Self will often cause you to make decisions that are 'best for you.' This does NOT mean doing whatever makes you happy or doing whatever you want to do! For example, you may want to eat a whole tub of ice cream, but you know that this behavior is not what is 'best for you' and the wisest choice is to avoid doing so. Unfortunately, people often get offended or hurt by our actions if what we are doing is best for us but not good for them. When doing what is best for you gets you called selfish or inconsiderate, try to remember that it is selfish for anyone to ask you to do what is best for them if it means you have to compromise the person you really Are.

TRUTH AND DARE

"Me vs. the me You want me to Be" Exercise

People pleasing Pat – a person who is highly committed to gaining the approval of others by doing and saying things to make others happy. A person who likes to be recognized and appreciated for every little thing they do and often try to convince people to like them with gifts, favors, or by appearing valuable to the person they are trying to get the approval of.

Fake Francis – having a false or misleading appearance; deceptive or not genuine. A person who is pretending to be someone or something they are normally not.

Sacrificing Sam – someone who goes without or suffers a loss so that someone else can gain or benefit from their action. Often these people think or feel that the other person is more worthy or deserving of whatever they are giving up.

Conforming Chris – a person who goes with the flow to avoid being different or unique. A conformer decides what to do based on what others are doing.

Agreeable Alex – acts agreeable when they really don't agree. A person who says they agree when they don't in order to avoid conflict or debate.

Identify which inauthentic personality is most likely responsible for each comment, thought, or event presented. Use the descriptions above to help you decide if it is PPP (people-pleasing Pat), FF (fake Francis), SS (sacrificing Sam), CC (conforming Chris), or AA (agreeable Alex). Then, fill in the blank with either PPP, FF, SS, CC, or AA.

_____ "My boyfriend is the captain of the football team and he is always hungry. Almost every day he ends up eating both his lunch and mine."

_____ You see a friend of yours, who claims they don't like smoking, at a party and they are pretending to be enjoying a cigarette.

_____ "Here are the answers to the math homework, I know you have plans tonight so I thought I would help you out by doing the work for you."

_____ At lunch time, everyone at the table is talking about how hard the English test was and how the teacher is just trying to fail the class. Even though you love the teacher and found the test to be easy, you say "Yeah – I know, what's up with that?"

_____ "If everyone else is going to skip the pep rally, I guess I should too."

_____ "My being here is making Billy uncomfortable, so I guess I should just leave the party so he can have fun."

_____ You and your friend just got out of a movie that you thought was horrible and they keep going on and on about how great it was. Then, they ask you if you think it was great too and you respond with "yeah, it was really good!"

_____ "I did your chores for you because I don't want you to get in trouble!"

_____ You notice a friend laughing at a joke being told by a guy or girl they think is cute even though you know that they didn't think it was funny.

_____ Even though you like wearing your shirt tucked in, you choose to wear it hanging out because that's how all your friends wear theirs.

Which of these 5 behaviors do you do most often? _____

Which two would you like to avoid the most? _____

\& _____

Dare 6

"Knowing others is wisdom, knowing yourself is Enlightenment."   ~Lao Tzu

Dare to know Who You Are by discovering who you are not.

If you were to ask someone, "Who Are You," you may be very surprised by the variety of different answers you can get. Some people define themselves by who they are in relation to other people, some may tell you what they do for a living, and others may begin to tell you their whole life story. However, none of these actually come close to answering the question. Instead of telling others Who We Are, we often refer to What We Are – Billy's brother, the school secretary, or the person who spilled milk on Joe in the 3rd grade. The reason so many people struggle with answering such a simple question is because they believe that they are something that they are not. Abraham Lincoln said it like this, "Character is like a tree and reputation like a shadow. The shadow is what we think of it; the tree is the real thing." The shadow in this analogy is our 'false self'- the person we pretend to be; it may be the person we think others want us to be (the victim) or who we think we ought to be (the ego). The tree is Who We Really Are; our authentic and True Self (the I). Truth is, getting to know and recognize your 'false self' is the surest and easiest way to know your True Self. To help you recognize and identify the difference between your false self and your True Self, we will use the phrase - 'me, Myself, and I.' Your 'me' is your victim self; this self is very child-like and often pessimistic. Your 'me' usually feels hurt, betrayed, rejected, unwanted, and helpless. Your 'Myself' is your ego self; this self is very competitive, judgmental, and controlling. Your 'Myself' often feels threatened by other's success, disrespected, under-valued, justified in their behaviors, and defensive. Both your 'me' and your 'Myself' are fear-driven false selves that share the goal of gaining and maintaining the approval and love of others. Your 'I' is your True Authentic Self; this Self is wise, optimistic, and always Loving. Your 'I' never feels a need to judge anyone or anything, including ItSelf. Unlike your 'me' and your 'myself,' your 'I' focuses on learning and personal growth, seeks only for Its own approval, and desires only to extend Love. Unfortunately, the victim and the ego will be quite familiar for most people and the 'I' may seem to be more like a fictional character that we only aspire to be like. However, as Sigmund Freud declared, "The ego is not master in its own house." The more aware we become of the 'false self' and our 'True Self,' the less likely we will be to allow fear to keep us from the joy, success, peace, and Love that we desire and deserve. Your 'I' knows that all these things are available to us because they live within US.

To accomplish this dare: Complete the "me, Myself, and I," and the "I AM" exercises on the following page. Then, use the I AM acronym to help you recognize when your me, Myself, and I make appearances throughout your day. For 3 days, try to record at least one appearance of each 'self' during that day and identify which 'self' shows up the most.

"me, Myself, and I" Exercise

For each of the following sentences, identify which self (me, Myself, or I) is most likely the self who would make that statement. For 'me,' use 1... 'Myself,' use 2... and 'I,' use 3.

_____ "No one ever invites me to go to the movies or hang out. That makes me sad."

_____ "Giving us a test the day after vacation is just wrong! I am not going to study."

_____ "Nothing I do ever makes my mom happy, I don't know why she is so hard on me."

_____ "I didn't make the team, but I really enjoyed trying out."

_____ "It is SO not fair that my brother got a brand new cell phone when his broke and I got my dad's old hand me down when I broke my phone."

_____ "I didn't do as well as my best friend did in the game today. I am happy my friend was recognized for his efforts. He deserved it."

_____ "People are always breaking up with me. There must be something wrong with me."

_____ "I just heard my friends talking poorly about me behind my back. I guess now is a good time for me to practice being forgiving and loyal."

_____ "You have been lying to me this whole time. There's NO way I can trust you now!"

Circle feelings that are typical for 'me.' Put a square around feelings typical for 'Myself.' Underline feelings typical for 'I'. (Try to find 7 for each)

Angry	Embarrassed	Valued	Offended	Accepted
Encouraged	Unwanted	Abused	Compassionate	Deceived
Depressed	Frustrated	Peaceful	Resentful	Optimistic
Ignored	Understanding	Wronged	Insulted	Hurt	Rejected

"I AM" Exercise

I: imagine yourself stepping into the back of your mind and becoming an observer of what is currently happening. Imagine that you are detached from the thoughts and emotions that the event is creating and try to visualize yourself, watching yourself, as the event continues.

A: acknowledge which self shows up to deal with the event. Is it 'me,' 'Myself,' or 'I'?

M: mentally identify how each of the 3 selves would respond to the event and make an effort to experience a little more 'I' time every day.

Practice example: Imagine that you're observing yourself being broken up with by someone you have been dating for over a year.

How would your 'me' respond? _____

How would your 'Myself' respond? _____

How would your 'I' respond? _____

Authenticity/Self Love Dare 1

It took (no effort / a little effort / more effort than I thought / a lot of effort) to let my actions speak for me and avoid trying to change other's opinions.

I (found / didn't find / found but didn't take) an opportunity to say "You have the right to your opinion and I don't feel the need to try and change it."

My 3 most common reactions/responses when someone doesn't like me, says negative things about me, or thinks something about me that isn't true are:

1.) _____

2.) _____

3.) _____

During the 3 days, the hardest thing I had to do was _____

_____

My normal response would have been to _____

and the result/response is usually _____

What positive and/or negative feelings did you experience when you allowed other's to form/ have their own opinions of you by avoiding the actions listed?

_____

_____

How can continuing to practice this dare benefit you _____

_____

What is the most important thing you learned from this dare? _____

_____

CONGRATULATIONS ON YOUR SUCCESS

ACCOMPLISHED
Authenticity/Self Love Dare 2

What message or lesson was the "What's good for You…is good for Me

Exercise" teaching? _____

How did the exercise make you feel? Mark them as T(true) or F(false).

_____ I felt frustrated when I realized how unkind and unloving I am to myself.

_____ I felt thankful for learning how I can be more loving and kind to myself.

_____ I felt motivated to be more loving and kind to myself.

_____ I felt disappointed in myself for thinking I was not as deserving as others.

Which 2 did you commit to doing for 3 days? _____

and _____

How successful were you at doing each of them? _____

_____

What are the benefits of doing each of them? _____

_____

Of the 11 actions, how many do you do often enough to call it a habit? _____

Which 2 did you choose to do the opposite of for 3 days and how did that go?

_____

_____

What would be the benefit of practicing this dare and being more loving to yourself

_____

CONGRATULATIONS ON YOUR SUCCESS

ACCOMPLISHED
Authenticity/Self Love Dare 3

How did doing the "It's Not FAIR to Compare" exercise make you feel? _____

_____

What was the most important thing you learned from the exercise? _____

_____

Record how you used the FAIR acronym on 1 of the 3 occasions.

What was the comparison being made? _____

_____

Were you feeling Greater Than or Less Than in the equation? _____

F: (List 2 reasons why the comparison may not have been fair) _____

_____

_____

A: (What did you acknowledge and appreciate) _____

_____

_____

I: (What did you identify as your highest potential) _____

_____

R: (What did you remember about your worth and value) _____

_____

CONGRATULATIONS ON YOUR SUCCESS

TRUTH AND DARE

ACCOMPLISHED

Authenticity/Self Love Dare 4

It was (impossible / very hard / hard / not too hard / easy) for me to go 2 consecutive days saying only what was worthy of being spoken.

When doing this dare, I was (silent / extremely quiet / a little more quiet than usual / as talkative as I normally am / _____)

Did anyone notice a difference in the amount or quality of what you were saying while doing this dare? Yes / No If Yes, what did they say? _____

_____

Did you examine what others were saying to see if it was worthy of being said? Yes / No

If Yes, what did you find? _____

I found that most of my thoughts were (worthy / unworthy) of being spoken.

When I did have to remain silent, it was most often because my words were not (honest / admirable / valuable / encouraging).

If I want people to listen to and value what I say, one thing I may need to work on is

_____

Two negative consequences that can come from frequently speaking unworthy or useless thoughts are:

1.) _____

2.) _____

The most important thing I learned from doing this dare was _____

_____

CONGRATULATIONS ON YOUR SUCCESS

Authenticity/Self Love Dare 5

After reading this dare, I can honestly say that I believe I am most like

(People Pleasing Pat / Fake Francis / Sacrificing Sam / Conforming Chris / Agreeable Alex)

because _____

_____

The personality I am least like is _____

The personality I least like in others would probably be _____

because _____

I believe that I (always / often / sometimes / rarely / never) pretend to be who others want me to be instead of just being myself.

I (always / often / sometimes / rarely / never) act differently in front of different people.

Who is the most authentic person you know? _____

How does being around this person make you feel? _____

Who is the most inauthentic person you know and why do you think this person appears

to be, or acts, fake? _____

_____

What do you think the greatest benefit would be of practicing watching out for these

personalities in your everyday life? _____

_____

TRUTH AND DARE

CONGRATULATIONS ON YOUR SUCCESS

ACCOMPLISHED
Authenticity/Self Love Dare 6

What did the "me, Myself, and I" exercise teach you? _____

_____

What did you learn from the "I AM" exercise? _____

_____

Which self is easiest for you to recognize and why? _____

_____

Which self shows up the most in your everyday life? _____

Which self shows up the least? _____

Did you notice if certain selves come out around certain people? Yes / No

If yes, who brings out which self every time you around them and why? _____

_____

Did you notice when other people's me, Myself, and I showed up? Yes / No

If Yes, which self did you see most often from others? _____

Of all the people you know, who do you see their 'me' the most? _____

Who is most often being their "I"? _____

How can continuing to practice this dare benefit you throughout your life? _____

_____

_____

CONGRATULATIONS ON YOUR SUCCESS

CHAPTER REVIEW

What is your favorite quote from this chapter? Why?

_____

_____

Which of the dares was the hardest? Why?

_____ because _____

_____

_____

Which of the dares was the easiest? Why?

_____ because _____

_____

_____

Which dare made you feel the best about what you had done? Why?

_____ because _____

_____

_____

Which dare do you think you will try to do most often? Why?

_____ because _____

_____

_____

Which dare did you do the most? # _____

Which dare did you do the least? # _____

Which dare was easiest to remember? # _____ hardest? # _____

Which dare had the most shocking/dramatic results? # _____ why? _____

_____

Which dare or dares did people seem to notice when you did it? _____

What did you learn about yourself and/or others through this chapter's exercises?

_____

_____

_____

_____

_____

_____

_____

Can you think of another way to dare yourself in order to test or build-up this virtue?

_____

_____

_____

_____

_____

_____

_____

_____

What was fun about these exercises? _____

_____

_____

What was not so fun? _____

_____

Use these 2 pages to keep notes during the week, jot down ideas or thoughts, or to evaluate your success. Set goals to help you accomplish the dares and goals for practicing them in the future.

_____

_____

_____

_____

_____

_____

_____

_____

_____

_____

_____

_____

_____

_____

_____

_____

_____

_____

_____

_____

_____

_____

_____

_____

_____

"It is not because things are difficult that we do not dare; it is because we do not dare that things are difficult."
$\sim$Seneca

"The most common form of despair
is not being who you are."

Soren Kierkegaard

"This above all; to thine own self be true."

William Shakespeare

CHAPTER 10

THE JOURNEY

Dear _____, (Please insert your name)

My name is Wendy Lynn and I am the creator/author of the Truth And Dare program. As you have probably noticed, I have made this program all about You! I have kept myself out of this book and completely hidden from you for a very good reason. However, I now want to explain why, and in doing so I am certain you will be able to see me for the person I AM. When I began writing the Truth And Dare program, I knew that I didn't want it to be just another book where an adult was telling a teen what they should do, shouldn't do, or need to do if they want to be a good, successful, and happy person. As a matter of fact, I couldn't do that even if I tried because when I started writing... I was not, in my own perspective, any of these things. I was not honest, respectful, generous, accepting, encouraging, appreciative, loyal, optimistic, or authentic. So, I thought to myself... "Who am I to write a book for teens to help them develop these virtues or qualities if I myself, at the age of 37, am unable to do so?" When I shared this thought with my life coach at the time, she asked me a question that eventually would change my life. She said to me, "Wendy, what makes you unable to be a virtuous, good, happy, and successful person?" As I sat there quietly for a few moments, so many thoughts and excuses ran through my head. "I never have been, so I never can be." "I don't know how to be." "It's too late to change; it's just not in my nature to be." It didn't take me long to realize that none of these thoughts, or better called excuses, were true at all. Just from that one question, I came to understand that I AM 'able' to be – I just 'choose' not to be virtuous, good, happy, and successful. At that moment, I made a new choice. I decided that I was going to change my behaviors to be more reflective of the kind of person I wanted to be. Then, maybe I would feel good enough about myself to write the program.

After 3 years of reading every book I could find on personal growth and practicing every day to be a more virtuous and honorable person, I still felt like a hypocrite. Even though I was much wiser and my behaviors had improved beyond what I thought was even possible, I still lived in the shadow of the person I had always been. Instead of seeing myself as a new and improved person, I saw myself as someone who had gotten pretty darn good at pretending to be a great person. Even though I still felt like a hypocrite, I started writing the program anyway. I felt confident that I had enough wisdom and experience to help others – even if I hadn't been able to help myself. It took me about three weeks to decide what I wanted the nine chapters to be about and another four weeks to find all the quotes that I needed to make the Truths clear and the Dares possible. Then, I began the most difficult and rewarding journey of my Life – Truth And Dare.

I want you to know that every dare in this program has had a powerful effect on my life. When I sat down to write each dare, I was scared of what I knew was coming. For me, Truth And Dare was like 'The School of Hard Knocks!' If I was writing a dare about forgiving others, people were certainly going to try and push my buttons so that I could practice what I was preaching. For the record, I often failed BIG TIME. Quite honestly, it frequently sucked! When I wrote the dare about appreciating nature and putting away electronical devices for a little while, within a few hours I had dropped and broken my $400 phone AND dropped my ipod in the bathtub. There were many days, and even months, when I wouldn't write at all because I was afraid of the challenges I knew I would have to face with the upcoming dares. I was very hard on myself when I wrote a dare and then failed to do what I knew was most beneficial when the challenges appeared. I felt more like a hypocrite now than I ever did before. But, I kept going. I think the little successes I had along the way gave me hope and encouraged me to continue forward. Yet, there was one quote that helped me when I was convinced that there was NO way I was going to keep writing. Ambrose Redmoon said, "Courage is not the absence of fear, but rather the judgment that something else is more important than fear." You – You were my something else. Whenever I thought that I couldn't take or go any more, I thought of YOU and wrote!

Now that the program is done being written, I can honestly say that I AM no longer a hypocrite! Have I mastered the dares in the program and are my behaviors and thoughts always in alignment with the highest and greatest Self? NO! However, I AM working on it. ;) I can honestly say that this program has awakened me to the Truth and has given me the tools and encouragement to change the person I was so ashamed to be. I AM a far more virtuous, loving, and accepting person today than I ever imagined I could BE, and I look forward to the Who I have yet to BEcome. Every day, I remind myself of the quote by e.e. cummings who said, "To be nobody but yourself in a world which is doing its best, night and day, to make you somebody else, means to fight the hardest battle which any human being can fight; and never stop fighting." I know the days ahead will have difficulties and I know that I will often fall short of Being the person I truly AM, as will you if you continue your journey. However, I am not willing to let my fears keep me from the Love and Life I desire and deserve. I know I can do this, and I believe you can as well. Joe Cordare once said, "To the question of your life, you are the answer; to the problems of your life, you are the solution." In other words, be sure to Live Your Own Life by Being your Authentic Self and believe in YourSelf by trusting your ability to get through the obstacles and challenges that Life brings you.

Throughout this program, I have presented many Truths for you to consider and have given you 54 dares to accomplish. Now it's your turn. On the following three pages, you will find a quote at the top of each page. From that quote, write your own Truth. Explain why you think the quote is true, important, and/or beneficial. Then, try to create an exercise or dare that you can do to help you 'experience' the benefits of living in accordance to that Truth. If you disagree with any of the 3 quotes I have provided, or have another quote you wish to use, feel free to replace the one that I provided with your own. Remember, Truth And Dare is, and always will be, Your journey. Thank You for letting me share My Journey with YOU!

Dare 1

"If you really put a small value on yourself, rest assured that the world will not raise your price."

~Unknown

"Self-worth comes from one thing – thinking that you are worthy."

~Wayne Dyer

Dare to _____ .

_____

_____

_____

_____

_____

_____

_____

_____

_____

_____

_____

_____

_____

_____

To accomplish this dare: _____

_____

_____

_____

_____

_____

_____

Dare 2

"Life isn't about finding yourself. Life is about creating YourSelf."

~George Bernard Shaw

"What you get by achieving your goals is not as important as what you Become by achieving your goals."

~Zig Ziglar

Dare to _____ .

_____

_____

_____

_____

_____

_____

_____

_____

_____

_____

_____

To accomplish this dare: _____

_____

_____

_____

_____

_____

Dare 3

"The shortest and surest way to live with honor in the world, is to BE in reality what we would appear to be; all human virtues increase and strengthen themselves by the practice and experience of them."
                                                                    ~Socrates

Dare to _____.

_____

_____

_____

_____

_____

_____

_____

_____

_____

_____

_____

_____

To accomplish this dare: _____

_____

_____

_____

_____

_____

_____

Wendy Lynn was born in New Orleans, Louisiana in 1969. At the age of 40, Wendy graduated, Summa Cum Laude, from the University of New Orleans with special focus in Psychology and Philosophy. In the fall of 2008, she received her Empowerment Life Coaching Certification from iPec (Institute for Professional Excellence in Coaching) and also completed the Life Potentials Certification Program.

Believing that the many struggles that both children and adults deal with *externally* are actually a direct result of their own personal *internal* battles, Wendy set out to create an empowerment coaching program that would not only expose the Truth of Who We Really Are, but also Dare us to find the courage to Be that person in a world that is constantly trying to make us into someone else. After living most of her life hiding behind the many social masks she had created to gain the acceptance, approval, and love of others, Wendy came to realize that being who she thought others wanted her to be was neither the easiest nor the best way to live. This Truth began her journey of Living her Life from the Inside-out. After successfully taking back her Life from the world around her, Wendy became passionate about empowering teens with the Self Acceptance, Self Respect, and Self Love that they both desired and deserved. The Truth And Dare program evolved from her decision to Create and Be the person she desired to Be instead of letting others determine what she would become. Sharing her journey and encouraging others to Be the Who They Are meant to Be has become Wendy's new Life Purpose.

For more information about Courses, Workshops, Services, and Products,

visit the Truth And Dare website:

www.truthanddare.org

CPSIA information can be obtained at www.ICGtesting.com
Printed in the USA
LVOW011429070512

280687LV00001B/5/P